DOLOMITES TRAVEL

GUIDE

A Comprehensive Travel companion to Unveil the Beauty, Adventure, and Hidden Gems of this Alpine Wonderland, Packed with Insider Tips for an Unforgettable Journey and Practical Insights to Maximize Your Experience and Budget.Copyright

NOAH HICKS
Travel Companion

TABLE OF CONTENT

HOW TO USE THIS GUIDE

Discover the allure of the Dolomites with a warm welcome and explore the Top 10 Reasons why this destination should be on your travel radar.

CHAPTER 1: OVERVIEW OF THE DOLOMITES

Unearth the rich History and Culture of the Dolomites, find the Best Things to Do, and explore Top Attractions that make this region truly captivating.

CHAPTER 2: DOLOMITES PACKING LIST

Prepare for your adventure with a detailed guide on What to Pack for a Trip to the Dolomites.

CHAPTER 3: EXPLORING THE DOLOMITES

Navigate festivals, gather Essential Tips for Traveling, understand Tourist Seasons, and grasp the ins and outs of Getting Around with Travel Rules and Regulations.

CHAPTER 4: CULINARY DELIGHTS OF THE DOLOMITES

Indulge your taste buds with insights into the Best Places to Eat, Must-Try Local Dishes, and the prime Shopping Spots in the Dolomites.

CHAPTER 5: ACCOMMODATION AND SCENIC SPOTS

Choose your stay wisely with tips on Where to Stay, explore the Best Scenic Spots, and find recommendations for Luxury and Budget-Friendly Accommodations.

CHAPTER 6: DAY TRIPS IN THE DOLOMITES

Plan your adventure with an Itinerary for a 7-Day Trip, ensuring you make the most of your time in this stunning region.

CHAPTER 7: MAKING THE MOST OF YOUR MONEY AND OUTDOOR ACTIVITIES

Optimize your budget with Money-Saving Tips, gain Insider Tips for Exploring, and dive into the plethora of Outdoor Activities the Dolomites offer.

CHAPTER 8: IMMERSING IN DOLOMITE CULTURE AND HERITAGE

Delve into the cultural scene with a tour of Museums and Galleries, explore Historical Sites and Landmarks, and experience Traditional Dolomite Music and Dance.

CHAPTER 9: HEALTH AND SAFETY IN THE DOLOMITES

Ensure a safe journey with Emergency Contacts, locate Healthcare Facilities, follow Safety Tips, and discover Recommended Apps and Websites for a secure travel experience.

ABOUT THE AUTHOR

Hello, **I'm Noah Hicks**, an avid explorer and your guide to the world's most captivating destinations. With a pen in hand and a heart set on discovery, I weave tales of travel that transport you to far-off lands. As your virtual companion, I navigate through bustling cities and serene landscapes, sharing the thrill of adventure and the warmth of cultural encounters.

Join me on a literary odyssey where the pages come alive with the sounds, smells, and sights of distant lands. Let's embark on a journey together, where every chapter sparks the wanderlust within you. I invite you to embrace the thrill of exploration and make your own unforgettable memories across the globe. The adventure begins with a turn of the page, and I'm here to guide you every step of the way

WELCOME TO DOLOMITES

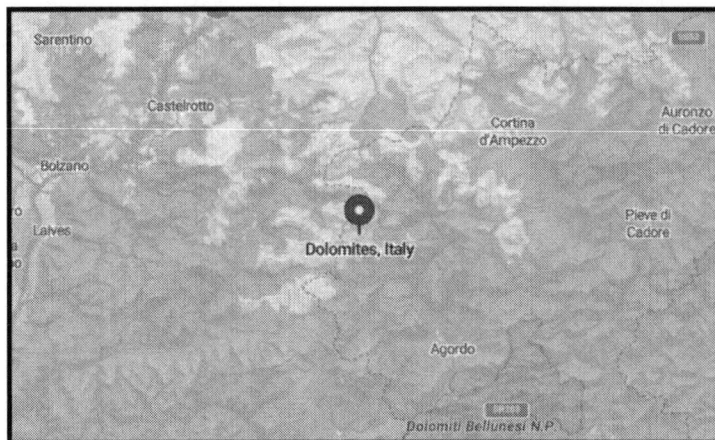

Welcome to the enchanting world of the Dolomites, where nature's grandeur meets cultural richness in a breathtaking fusion. As you embark on this journey through our guide, envision yourself surrounded by the majestic peaks, verdant valleys, and a tapestry of experiences that define the Dolomites.

It as a trusted companion, offering insights, tips, and suggestions to make your Dolomite adventure seamless and unforgettable. Whether you're a nature enthusiast, history buff, or a seeker of culinary delights, the Dolomites have something extraordinary to offer.

Now, let's take a glimpse into what this guide has in store for you. It's more than a mere collection of facts; it's a roadmap to tailor your Dolomite experience to perfection.

Imagine flipping through the pages and discovering the rich history and culture that lays the foundation for the Dolomites. Uncover the Best Things to Do, guiding you to experiences that capture the essence of this remarkable region. Top Attractions await your exploration, promising moments that will linger in your memories.

As you plan your Dolomite adventure, our guide extends a helpful hand in Chapter 2, providing insights into the essentials with the Dolomites Packing List. This section ensures you're well-prepared, letting you focus on the beauty around you.

Chapter 3 takes you deep into the heart of the Dolomites, revealing the secrets of festivals, essential travel tips, and the nuances of navigating through the region. Understand the Tourist Seasons and acquaint yourself with the rules and regulations, ensuring a smooth and respectful journey.

Your gastronomic journey begins in Chapter 4, where we guide you to the Best Places to Eat, introduce you to Must-Try Local Dishes and Drinks, and point you towards the prime Shopping Spots in the Dolomites.

Accommodation becomes an art in Chapter 5, where we assist you in choosing the perfect stay. Discover the Best Scenic Spots, and explore options ranging from luxurious retreats to budget-friendly accommodations, all tailored to your preferences.

The adventure doesn't stop there. Chapter 6 unveils a curated Itinerary for a 7-Day Trip, providing a comprehensive plan to make the most of your time in the Dolomites.

Chapter 7 is your gateway to financial savvy and outdoor thrills. Maximize your budget with Money-Saving Tips, gain Insider Insights for Exploring, and immerse yourself in a spectrum of Outdoor Activities that the Dolomites offer.

Cultural aficionados will find Chapter 8 a treasure trove, guiding you through Museums and Galleries, Historical Sites and Landmarks, and the soul-stirring notes of Traditional Dolomite Music and Dance.

Safety is paramount, and Chapter 9 ensures your well-being. Discover Emergency Contacts, locate Healthcare Facilities, absorb Safety Tips, and equip yourself with Recommended Apps and Websites for a secure travel experience.

This guide is your passport to an unforgettable Dolomite adventure. As you turn the pages, feel the excitement building, envision the stunning landscapes, and anticipate the extraordinary experiences awaiting you. It's not just a guide; it's your gateway to a journey where every moment is a brushstroke on the canvas of your Dolomite adventure.

Now, let curiosity be your guide. Explore further, dive into the chapters that resonate with your wanderlust, and begin crafting the itinerary for your Dolomite escapade. The Dolomites await, and this guide is your trusted companion in unlocking its wonders. Happy exploring!

Reasons to Visit the Dolomites

Nestled in the heart of the Italian Alps, the Dolomites stand as a testament to nature's grandeur and cultural richness, offering a compelling array of reasons to make it your next travel destination.

1. Majestic Peaks and Breathtaking Landscapes

The Dolomites boast a collection of towering peaks and breathtaking landscapes that defy imagination. These UNESCO World Heritage-listed mountains captivate with their sheer cliffs, rugged ridges, and alpine meadows, creating a visual symphony that unfolds in every direction.

2. Outdoor Adventures for Every Season:

Whether you're an adrenaline junkie or a nature enthusiast, the Dolomites cater to all. From exhilarating ski slopes in winter to captivating hiking trails in summer, this destination seamlessly blends adventure and tranquility throughout the year. Embrace the thrill of rock climbing, cycling, or simply savor the serenity of a leisurely stroll amid pristine nature.

3. Rich Cultural Heritage:

Beyond the natural wonders, the Dolomites harbor a rich cultural heritage. Explore ancient villages, each telling a story through its architecture and traditions. Engage with the warm local communities, where centuries-old customs and festivals are woven into the fabric of daily life.

4. Unparalleled Skiing and Winter Sports:
For winter enthusiasts, the Dolomites offer a skiing paradise. Renowned ski resorts like Cortina d'Ampezzo and Alta Badia beckon with perfectly groomed slopes, panoramic views, and a winter wonderland ambiance. Whether you're a seasoned skier or a novice, the Dolomites provide an unforgettable snowy escapade.

5. Scenic Drives and Picturesque Villages:
The Dolomites are a dream for road-trippers. Scenic drives wind through mountain passes, unveiling jaw-dropping vistas at every turn. Discover charming villages like Ortisei, Cortina, and Castelrotto, each with its own unique charm, nestled against the backdrop of the awe-inspiring peaks.

6. World-Class Culinary Experiences:

Indulge your taste buds in the delectable offerings of Dolomite cuisine. Savory dishes featuring local ingredients, artisanal cheeses, and hearty Alpine flavors define the gastronomic scene. Immerse yourself in rustic mountain huts or elegant restaurants to savor the unique culinary delights of the region.

7. Photographer's Paradise:

For photographers, the Dolomites are a dream canvas. Sunrise and sunset transform the mountains into a kaleidoscope of colors, creating a mesmerizing spectacle that demands to be captured. The play of light and shadow on the rock faces creates a dynamic visual symphony, making every frame a work of art.

8. Wellness Retreats Amid Nature:

Escape the hustle and bustle of daily life in the Dolomites' serene wellness retreats. Rejuvenate mind and body in spa resorts that seamlessly integrate with the natural surroundings, offering relaxation against a backdrop of unparalleled beauty.

9. Hiking Trails for All Levels:

Whether you're a seasoned trekker or a casual hiker, the Dolomites offer a network of trails catering to all levels. Explore the famous Alta Via routes or opt for gentle paths that lead to hidden alpine lakes, ensuring that every step is a discovery.

10. Stargazing in the Clear Alpine Sky:
As night falls, the Dolomites unveil a celestial spectacle. Away from urban lights, the clear Alpine sky provides a mesmerizing canvas for stargazers. Lay back and be enchanted by a blanket of stars, adding a celestial touch to your Dolomite experience.

CHAPTER 1

OVERVIEW OF THE
DOLOMITES

History and culture

Welcome, fellow adventurers! I'm excited to guide you through the enchanting landscapes of the Dolomites – a realm where nature unfolds its most dramatic and captivating scenes. As the author of this travel guide, my goal is simple: to immerse you in the allure of the Dolomites, sharing firsthand experiences and insights gained from traversing these awe-inspiring mountains.

Close your eyes and imagine a landscape sculpted by the hands of giants – towering peaks that punctuate the skyline, valleys adorned with vibrant flora, and trails that beckon the curious soul. This is the Dolomites, a destination that transcends mere description. Through the pages of this guide, I aim to paint a vivid picture of this alpine wonderland, capturing the essence of its rugged beauty.

Consider this guide not as a handbook but as a personal invitation to explore the Dolomites. Picture yourself alongside me, venturing into the heart of these mountains, breathing in the crisp mountain air, and witnessing the play of light on the majestic peaks. What unfolds is not just a journey through a geographic marvel but an immersion into an experience that resonates with the spirit of adventure.

As you turn the pages, expect more than a recitation of facts. This guide is an extension of my personal diary, filled with anecdotes and discoveries that shaped my understanding of the Dolomites. Each chapter unveils a facet of this alpine tapestry, inviting you to delve deeper into its mysteries.

Let's talk about the peaks – those sentinels that define the Dolomites. They rise with an imposing grandeur, their rugged outlines contrasting against the boundless sky. From the iconic Tre Cime di Lavaredo to the lesser-known gems like the Tofane and the Marmolada, each summit has a story to tell. Through my experiences, you'll gain insights into the best vantage points, the thrill of reaching a summit, and the quietude that descends as you stand atop these giants.

Venturing beyond the heights, the Dolomites reveal a network of trails that weave through meadows, forests, and alpine lakes. It's not just about conquering peaks but about the journey itself. I'll guide you through the most scenic trails, share tips on navigating the terrain, and highlight the hidden gems that await those willing to explore off the beaten path.

Now, let's talk culture. The Dolomites aren't just a canvas of natural wonders; they are also steeped in history and tradition. From charming mountain villages to centuries-old traditions, the human element adds a rich layer to this alpine saga. You'll discover the warmth of local hospitality, savor traditional Alpine cuisine, and perhaps stumble upon a festive celebration that echoes through the valleys.

In your exploration, you'll encounter the delicate dance between light and rock that transforms these mountains into a kaleidoscope of colors. Sunrise and sunset become magical moments, painting the peaks with hues of pink, orange, and purple. My guide will provide tips on capturing these fleeting spectacles, ensuring that your memories are not just etched in your mind but also preserved in photographs.

As you leaf through the guide, practical details will seamlessly blend with narrative, offering a holistic approach to planning your Dolomite adventure. Accommodation recommendations, dining insights, and tips on transportation will help you navigate the logistics, allowing you to focus on the sheer joy of exploration.

Best Things to Do in the Dolomites

In the heart of the Italian Alps, the Dolomites beckon with a wealth of experiences that cater to nature lovers, adventure seekers, and culture enthusiasts alike. As you navigate through this alpine wonderland, here's a curated list of the best things to do, ensuring your journey through the Dolomites is nothing short of extraordinary.

Explore Majestic Peaks and Panoramic Views

Begin your Dolomite adventure by immersing yourself in the breathtaking vistas that define this region. The towering peaks, notably Tre Cime di Lavaredo, offer a jaw-dropping panorama. Hike or drive to strategic viewpoints like Passo Pordoi or Seceda for an awe-inspiring perspective, where the interplay of light and shadow on the rugged peaks creates a visual symphony.

Conquer the Alta Via Routes

For avid hikers, the Dolomites present the famed Alta Via trails. These long-distance routes traverse the region, offering a trekking experience like no other. Each route varies in difficulty, but all promise encounters with pristine landscapes, alpine meadows, and the sheer beauty of the Dolomite wilderness.

Ski the Renowned Slopes

Winter transforms the Dolomites into a snowy paradise, and skiing enthusiasts find themselves in a haven of world-class slopes. Head to popular resorts like Cortina d'Ampezzo, Alta Badia, or Val Gardena for a skiing experience that combines thrilling descents with captivating mountain views.

Visit Charming Alpine Villages

Discover the charm of the Dolomite villages, each with its unique character. Wander through the cobbled streets of Ortisei, with its wooden chalets and vibrant market squares. Explore the medieval appeal of Castelrotto, or embrace the glamour of Cortina d'Ampezzo, known as the "Queen of the Dolomites."

Experience the Sellaronda Circuit

For cyclists and motorbike enthusiasts, the Sellaronda circuit is a must-do. This scenic loop around the Sella massif offers stunning mountainous landscapes and takes you through high mountain passes, charming villages, and verdant valleys.

Delight in Local Cuisine

Savor the flavors of the Dolomites by indulging in the local cuisine. Try hearty dishes like canederli (dumplings), polenta, and speck (smoked ham). Pair your meal with a glass of regional wine, and don't forget to sample local cheeses like Puzzone di Moena. Embrace the culinary traditions that have been perfected in this alpine haven.

Discover the Enrosadira Phenomenon
Witness the magical Enrosadira phenomenon during sunset. As the sun dips below the horizon, the Dolomite peaks are bathed in hues of pink and purple, creating a mesmerizing spectacle. Seek out strategic viewpoints in the late afternoon and experience nature's own light show.

Visit the Iconic Lake Braies
Lake Braies, with its emerald waters surrounded by pine forests and the towering Seekofel mountain, is an iconic destination. Rent a rowboat and leisurely paddle across the lake or take a stroll along the scenic shoreline. The picturesque setting makes it a favorite spot for photographers and nature enthusiasts.

Marvel at the Giau Pass
Embark on a scenic drive through the Giau Pass, one of the most stunning mountain passes in the Dolomites. As you

navigate the winding road, revel in the dramatic landscapes featuring sharp peaks, lush meadows, and an ever-changing alpine backdrop.

Immerse Yourself in Ladin Culture

Embrace the unique Ladin culture of the Dolomites. Visit Ladin museums, attend local festivals, and interact with the warm and hospitable Ladin people. Their distinct language, customs, and traditions add a layer of authenticity to your Dolomite experience.

Hike to the Cinque Torri

The Cinque Torri, or Five Towers, is a cluster of rock formations that have become an iconic symbol of the Dolomites. Hike to this natural marvel, where the jagged spires create a dramatic silhouette against the sky. It's not just a geological wonder but also a haven for rock climbers seeking adventure.

Top Attractions to Visit

To ensure you make the most of your Dolomite adventure, we've curated a guide to the top attractions, complete with essential details for your convenience.

1. Tre Cime di Lavaredo

Opening Hours: Open year-round; specific hiking routes may be weather-dependent.

- Contact: Tre Cime di Lavaredo, 32041 Auronzo di Cadore BL, Italy
- Phone Number: +39 0435 39110

Tre Cime di Lavaredo, or the Three Peaks of Lavaredo, stands as an iconic symbol of the Dolomites. These distinctive towering spires attract hikers, climbers, and nature enthusiasts. The jagged peaks create a breathtaking backdrop, and the surrounding trails offer various vantage points to soak in the awe-inspiring landscapes.

2. Lake Braies

- Admission Fee: Free access to the lake area; boat rental fees apply.
- Contact: Lake Braies, 39030 Braies BZ, Italy
- Phone Number: +39 0474 748685

Lake Braies, with its crystal-clear waters nestled against a stunning mountainous backdrop, is a must-visit attraction. Take a leisurely stroll along the shoreline, rent a rowboat to explore the lake's tranquil waters, or simply bask in the serenity of this picturesque alpine gem.

3. Seceda

- Admission Fee: Cable car fees apply for round-trip rides.
- Contact: Seceda, 39046 Ortisei BZ, Italy
- Phone Number: +39 0471 777900

Seceda offers panoramic views that will leave you breathless. Reachable by cable car, the summit provides a sweeping vista of the surrounding peaks and valleys. Whether you're an avid photographer or simply seeking a moment of tranquility, Seceda is a top attraction not to be missed.

4. Cinque Torri

- Contact: Cinque Torri, 32043 Cortina d'Ampezzo BL, Italy

- Phone Number: +39 0436 4711

The Cinque Torri, or Five Towers, stand as a testament to nature's artistry. These distinctive rock formations offer a captivating backdrop for hikers and climbers. Explore the surrounding trails or join a guided tour to delve into the geological wonders and historical significance of this unique attraction.

Navigating the Dolomites to explore these top attractions is an adventure in itself. While each site may have its transportation options, the region is best explored by car, allowing you the flexibility to reach remote destinations and enjoy scenic drives. Public transportation, such as buses and cable cars, also connects major points of interest, ensuring accessibility for all visitors.

CHAPTER 2

DOLOMITES PACKING LIST

What to Pack for a Trip to the Dolomites

Before diving into season-specific items, here are some essentials for any Dolomites trip:
- Comfortable Hiking Boots: Sturdy footwear is crucial for exploring the diverse landscapes.
- Weather-Appropriate Clothing: Layers are key. Pack lightweight for summer, and insulating layers for winter.

- Backpack: A reliable daypack for hikes and excursions.

- Waterproof Jacket: Dolomites weather can be unpredictable, so be prepared for rain.

- Reusable Water Bottle: Stay hydrated during your outdoor adventures.

Spring (April - June)

1. Light Jacket: Evenings can be cool, especially at higher altitudes.

2. Rain Gear: Spring showers are common, so pack a compact rain jacket.

3. Wildflower Guidebook: Spring brings colorful blooms, and identifying flowers can add to your experience.

4. Sunscreen: The sun is gaining strength; protect your skin during long hikes.

Summer (July - August)

1. Sun Hat and Sunglasses: Shield yourself from the strong summer sun.

2. Light Clothing: T-shirts, shorts, and breathable fabrics are essential for warm days.

3. Swimwear: Enjoy the lakes and rivers for a refreshing dip.

4. Insect Repellent: Summer brings out insects; stay bite-free during your outdoor activities.

Autumn (September - November)

1. Warmer Layers: Temperatures can drop, especially in the evenings.

2. Fall Colors Guide: Witness the stunning foliage; a guidebook can enhance your appreciation.

3. Gloves and Hat: Be prepared for cooler mornings and evenings.

4. Camera: Capture the vibrant autumn hues.

Winter (December - March)

1. Insulated Jacket: Stay warm in the chilly winter air.

2. Thermal Layers: Dress in layers to retain heat during snowy excursions.

3. Snow Gear: If you plan on skiing or snowboarding, ensure you have the appropriate equipment.

4. Hand and Foot Warmers: Combat the cold with these handy additions.

All Seasons

1. Camera and Binoculars: Capture the breathtaking landscapes and observe local wildlife.

2. Power Bank: Keep devices charged, especially if relying on navigation apps.

3. First Aid Kit: Include basic supplies for minor injuries.

4. Language Guidebook: Learn basic Italian or Ladin phrases to enhance your cultural experience.

Packing for the Dolomites requires thoughtful consideration of the seasonal variations. Whether you're exploring in spring, summer, autumn, or winter, this comprehensive guide ensures you're well-prepared for an unforgettable adventure in this stunning mountain region. Enjoy your travels!

CHAPTER 3

EXPLORING THE DOLOMITES

Festivals in the Dolomites

Regenerate in the Dolomites, immersing yourself in the natural beauty that permeates this Alpine region. Let the majestic mountains breathe life into your senses, offering a retreat for your mind, body, and soul.

Embark on hiking and nature walks, traversing the intricate network of trails that wind through the Dolomites. Whether opting for a leisurely stroll or a challenging hike, the diverse landscapes provide an opportunity to reconnect with nature. Inhale the crisp mountain air, and let the surroundings invigorate your spirit.

Discover the tranquility of alpine lakes such as Lago di Braies and Lago di Sorapis. These pristine bodies of water mirror the surrounding peaks, creating a serene backdrop for moments of reflection. As you bask in the quietude, let the beauty of the lakeside views soothe your soul.

Unwind in wellness retreats scattered across the Dolomites. Nestled amidst the mountains, these retreats offer spa facilities with panoramic views. Treat yourself to massages, yoga sessions, and thermal baths, allowing the therapeutic ambiance of the mountains to enhance your overall well-being.

Delve into the local cuisine, savoring the culinary delights that define the Dolomite experience. Indulge in South Tyrolean specialties, from hearty dumplings to exquisite cured meats.

The flavors of the region provide a sensory journey, complementing the natural splendor that surrounds you.

Participate in the Dolomiti Balloon Festival, where hot air balloons gracefully ascend against the backdrop of the Dolomite mountains. This mesmerizing spectacle offers a unique perspective of the landscapes below, adding a touch of magic to the serene winter skies.

Immerse yourself in the cultural tapestry of the Dolomites by attending festivals that celebrate the region's heritage. From the Alta Badia Food Festival to the Mareo Gherdëina ski race, these events offer a vibrant blend of traditions, music, and sports. Engaging with the local festivities provides a deeper connection to the people and the rich cultural fabric of the Dolomite communities.

Engage in winter sports, taking advantage of the snow-covered landscapes that define the colder months. Whether skiing, snowboarding, or simply relishing in the snowy ambiance, the Dolomites offer a playground for winter enthusiasts. Equip yourself with the necessary gear and embrace the thrill of winter activities against the backdrop of the majestic peaks.

Essential Tips for Traveling in the Dolomites

Regenerate in the Dolomites, immersing yourself in the natural beauty that permeates this Alpine region. Let the majestic mountains breathe life into your senses, offering a retreat for your mind, body, and soul.

Embark on hiking and nature walks, traversing the intricate network of trails that wind through the Dolomites. Whether opting for a leisurely stroll or a challenging hike, the diverse landscapes provide an opportunity to reconnect with nature. Inhale the crisp mountain air, and let the surroundings invigorate your spirit.

Discover the tranquility of alpine lakes such as Lago di Braies and Lago di Sorapis. These pristine bodies of water mirror the surrounding peaks, creating a serene backdrop for moments of reflection. As you bask in the quietude, let the beauty of the lakeside views soothe your soul.

Unwind in wellness retreats scattered across the Dolomites. Nestled amidst the mountains, these retreats offer spa facilities with panoramic views. Treat yourself to massages, yoga sessions, and thermal baths, allowing the therapeutic ambiance of the mountains to enhance your overall well-being.

Delve into the local cuisine, savoring the culinary delights that define the Dolomite experience. Indulge in South Tyrolean specialties, from hearty dumplings to exquisite cured meats. The flavors of the region provide a sensory journey, complementing the natural splendor that surrounds you.

Participate in the Dolomiti Balloon Festival, where hot air balloons gracefully ascend against the backdrop of the Dolomite mountains. This mesmerizing spectacle offers a unique perspective of the landscapes below, adding a touch of magic to the serene winter skies.

Immerse yourself in the cultural tapestry of the Dolomites by attending festivals that celebrate the region's heritage. From the Alta Badia Food Festival to the Mareo Gherdëina ski race, these events offer a vibrant blend of traditions, music, and sports. Engaging with the local festivities provides a deeper connection to the people and the rich cultural fabric of the Dolomite communities.

Engage in winter sports, taking advantage of the snow-covered landscapes that define the colder months. Whether skiing, snowboarding, or simply relishing in the snowy ambiance, the Dolomites offer a playground for winter enthusiasts. Equip yourself with the necessary gear and embrace the thrill of winter activities against the backdrop of the majestic peaks.

The Dolomites beckon with opportunities for rejuvenation and exploration. Whether you find solace in the tranquility of alpine lakes, seek wellness in mountain retreats, or embrace the thrill of outdoor activities, this region invites you to recharge amidst its breathtaking landscapes. Let the Dolomites be your sanctuary, where nature and culture converge to create an unforgettable experience for the senses.

Getting Around the Dolomites

To truly immerse yourself in this stunning region, exploring by various means of transportation is essential. Here's a guide to getting around the Dolomites to make the most of your adventure.

1. Car Rental

Renting a car provides unparalleled freedom to explore the Dolomites at your own pace. With well-maintained roads and awe-inspiring scenery, driving through mountain passes like the iconic Sella Ronda is a must. Ensure your rental vehicle is equipped for mountainous terrain, and be prepared for winding roads that showcase the Dolomites' dramatic landscapes.

2. Public Transportation

For a more environmentally conscious approach, the Dolomites boast an efficient public transportation system. Buses connect major towns, offering a convenient way to reach trailheads and picturesque spots. The Dolomiti Bus network is a reliable option for those wanting to reduce their carbon footprint while taking in the region's beauty.

3. Cable Cars and Gondolas

To reach higher altitudes without the strenuous hike, utilize the extensive network of cable cars and gondolas. These transport systems provide quick access to panoramic viewpoints and alpine meadows. Must-try ascents include the Seceda and Pordoi cable cars, offering unparalleled vistas of the Dolomite peaks.

4. Mountain Biking

For the more adventurous traveler, exploring the Dolomites on two wheels is an exhilarating experience. A network of mountain biking trails crisscrosses the region, offering varying difficulty levels. Rent a bike locally or bring your own to traverse scenic routes that lead through charming villages and dense forests.

5. Hiking: Step Into Nature's Embrace

Immerse yourself in the Dolomites' beauty by embarking on one of its numerous hiking trails. From gentle strolls to challenging treks, the region caters to all skill levels. Popular routes include the Alta Via 1 and 2, showcasing the Dolomites' diverse landscapes, from alpine meadows to rugged peaks.

6. E-Bikes: Effortless Exploration

For a more leisurely approach to mountain biking, consider renting an e-bike. These electrically assisted bicycles make navigating the hilly terrain more accessible, allowing you to cover more ground while still enjoying the breathtaking scenery. Many rental shops in the Dolomites offer e-bikes, making it a convenient option for all ages.

7. Skiing: Winter Wonderland Wonders

During the winter months, the Dolomites transform into a snowy wonderland, attracting ski enthusiasts from around the globe. A well-developed network of ski lifts and slopes caters to all skill levels. Whether you're a seasoned skier or a novice, the Dolomites offer an unforgettable winter sports experience.

8. Train Journeys: Scenic Routes

For a unique perspective of the Dolomites, embark on scenic train journeys. The region is well-connected by rail, allowing you to relax and enjoy the views while traversing the picturesque landscapes. The Bolzano to Cortina d'Ampezzo route is particularly renowned for its breathtaking vistas.

9. Horseback Riding: Serene Exploration

Experience the Dolomites from a different vantage point by exploring on horseback. Several stables in the region offer guided horseback riding excursions, allowing you to meander through meadows, forests, and charming villages while appreciating the tranquility of the surroundings.

10. Shuttle Services: Convenient Connections
To simplify your travels between towns and trailheads, take advantage of shuttle services. Many hotels and outdoor activity providers offer shuttle options, ensuring convenient connections and eliminating the hassle of navigating unfamiliar roads.

Travel Rules and Regulations in the Dolomites

From entry requirements to environmental conservation measures, here's a comprehensive guide to ensure you make the most of your visit while respecting the beauty and uniqueness of this Alpine wonderland.

1. Entry Requirements: Crossing Borders with Ease
Before setting foot in the Dolomites, familiarize yourself with Italy's entry requirements. Ensure your passport is valid for at

least six months beyond your planned departure date and check if a visa is necessary based on your nationality. Additionally, stay informed about any specific COVID-19-related protocols or restrictions that may be in place, as these can change periodically.

2. National Park Regulations: Preserving Pristine Landscapes

A significant portion of the Dolomites is protected within national parks, emphasizing the need for responsible tourism. Abide by park regulations, which may include designated trails, restricted areas, and waste disposal guidelines. Respect the delicate ecosystems and wildlife by staying on marked paths, refraining from littering, and adhering to any seasonal closures.

3. Accommodation Permits: Planning Your Stay

Certain areas within the Dolomites, especially those with limited access, may require special permits for overnight stays. This is particularly relevant for backcountry huts and camping spots. Check in advance whether your chosen accommodations necessitate permits and secure them accordingly to avoid any last-minute complications.

4. Wildlife Protection: Observe, Don't Disturb

The Dolomites are home to diverse wildlife, including chamois, ibexes, and golden eagles. When exploring, maintain a respectful distance and refrain from feeding or disturbing the animals. Follow guidelines provided by park authorities to ensure the preservation of the region's natural balance and to contribute to the sustainability of its ecosystems.

5. Waste Management: Leave No Trace

Preserving the pristine landscapes of the Dolomites relies on responsible waste management. Carry a reusable water bottle and snacks to minimize single-use plastic waste. Dispose of garbage in designated bins and, if necessary, pack out any non-biodegradable waste. Following the "Leave No Trace" principles ensures that future generations can continue to enjoy the beauty of the Dolomites.

6. Cultural Respect: Embracing Local Traditions

As you explore the charming villages and towns surrounding the Dolomites, take a moment to understand and respect the local culture. Follow dress codes when visiting religious sites, ask for permission before taking photographs of residents, and engage with the community in a considerate manner.

Embracing local traditions enhances your travel experience and fosters positive interactions.

7. Transportation Regulations: Navigating the Routes
Whether you're driving through mountain passes or utilizing public transportation, be aware of specific regulations. Mountain roads may have speed limits, and certain areas may require permits or reservations for private vehicles. Stay informed about road conditions, especially during winter when snowfall can impact travel plans.

8. Trail Etiquette: Sharing the Paths
The Dolomites offer an extensive network of hiking and biking trails, attracting outdoor enthusiasts from around the world. Practice good trail etiquette by yielding to uphill hikers, staying on marked paths, and avoiding shortcuts that can erode the landscape. Follow any specific rules posted at trailheads to ensure a harmonious experience for all visitors.

9. Winter Sports Guidelines: Safety First
If you're visiting the Dolomites during the winter months for skiing or snowboarding, familiarize yourself with safety guidelines. Observe avalanche warnings, use designated

slopes, and respect signage indicating closed areas. Adhering to these guidelines promotes a safe and enjoyable winter sports experience.

10. Emergency Contacts: Be Prepared

Finally, always have emergency contacts and local authorities' numbers on hand. Familiarize yourself with the location of medical facilities, ranger stations, and emergency services. Being prepared ensures a swift response in case of unforeseen circumstances and contributes to the overall safety of your adventure in the Dolomites.

CHAPTER 4

CULINARY DELIGHTS OF THE DOLOMITES

Best Places to Eat in the Dolomites

The Dolomites, with their stunning mountain landscapes and charming alpine villages, are not only a paradise for outdoor enthusiasts but also a culinary delight. From cozy mountain huts serving hearty traditional dishes to gourmet restaurants offering innovative cuisine, the Dolomites have something to satisfy every palate. Here are some of the best places to eat in the Dolomites, along with their opening hours, admissions fees (if applicable), contact information, and addresses:

1. Rifugio Scoiattoli
- Opening Hours: 9:00 am - 6:00 pm
- Admissions Fee: None
- Contact: +39 0471 849 422
- Address: Località Passo Falzarego, 32043 Cortina d'Ampezzo BL, Italy

Nestled at the foot of the iconic Cinque Torri rock formation, Rifugio Scoiattoli offers breathtaking views and delicious traditional cuisine. Enjoy a hearty plate of polenta with mushrooms or a steaming bowl of barley soup while taking in the stunning surroundings.

2. Rifugio Comici
- Opening Hours: 10:00 am - 5:00 pm
- Admissions Fee: None
- Contact: +39 0471 849 422

- Address: Località Passo Falzarego, 32043 Cortina d'Ampezzo BL, Italy

Located near the Falzarego Pass, Rifugio Comici is a popular spot for hikers and skiers looking to refuel with tasty mountain fare. Try their homemade pasta dishes or sample their selection of local cheeses and cured meats.

3. Rifugio Lagazuoi
- Opening Hours: 9:00 am - 5:00 pm
- Admissions Fee: None
- Contact: +39 0471 830292
- Address: Località Passo Falzarego, 32043 Cortina d'Ampezzo BL, Italy

Perched on the summit of Mount Lagazuoi, this rifugio offers panoramic views of the Dolomites and a menu featuring traditional Tyrolean specialties. Don't miss the opportunity to try their famous apple strudel paired with a steaming cup of mulled wine.

4. El Brite de Larieto
- Opening Hours: 12:00 pm - 3:00 pm, 7:00 pm - 10:00 pm

- Admissions Fee: None
- Contact: +39 0436 79107
- Address: Via Larieto, 2, 32020 Colle Santa Lucia BL, Italy

For a taste of gourmet cuisine in a cozy setting, head to El Brite de Larieto in the picturesque village of Colle Santa Lucia. Chef Matteo Metullio's creative dishes showcase the best of local ingredients and flavors, making this restaurant a must-visit for food lovers.

5. Ristorante Tivoli
- Opening Hours: 12:00 pm - 2:30 pm, 7:00 pm - 10:00 pm
- Admissions Fee: None
- Contact: +39 0436 867225
- Address: Via G. Marconi, 7, 32020 Selva di Cadore BL, Italy

Situated in the charming village of Selva di Cadore, Ristorante Tivoli is known for its warm hospitality and delicious Venetian cuisine. Indulge in dishes like risotto with porcini mushrooms or grilled sea bass while enjoying the cozy ambiance of this family-run restaurant.

6. Rifugio Fuciade

- Opening Hours: 9:00 am - 5:00 pm
- Admissions Fee: None
- Contact: +39 0437 599034
- Address: Strada de Fuciade, 38036 Canazei TN, Italy

Located in the heart of the Fassa Valley, Rifugio Fuciade is a favorite among hikers and skiers for its welcoming atmosphere and mouthwatering regional dishes. Try their hearty soups, grilled meats, and homemade desserts for a true taste of the Dolomites.

7. Albergo Ristorante Alpino

- Opening Hours: 12:00 pm - 2:30 pm, 7:00 pm - 10:00 pm
- Admissions Fee: None
- Contact: +39 0437 720130
- Address: Via Roma, 23, 38035 Moena TN, Italy

For a cozy dining experience in the charming town of Moena, look no further than Albergo Ristorante Alpino. This family-run restaurant serves up traditional Trentino dishes with a modern twist, using locally sourced ingredients to create unforgettable flavors.

Whether you're craving hearty mountain fare or gourmet cuisine, the Dolomites offer a culinary experience like no other. From rustic rifugios to fine dining restaurants, there's something to suit every taste and budget in this stunning alpine region. So pack your appetite and get ready to indulge in the delicious flavors of the Dolomites!

Must-Try Local Dishes and Drinks in the Dolomites

When visiting the Dolomites, one cannot miss the opportunity to indulge in the delicious local dishes and drinks that showcase the unique flavors of this alpine region. From hearty mountain fare to sweet treats, the Dolomites offer a culinary experience that is sure to tantalize your taste buds. Here are some must-try local dishes and drinks in the Dolomites:

1. Speck: A traditional cured meat that is a specialty of the South Tyrol region, speck is made from pork leg that is seasoned with salt, pepper, juniper, and other spices before being smoked and aged. This savory and slightly smoky meat is often sliced thinly and served as an appetizer or paired with cheese and bread.

2. Canederli: Also known as knödel or dumplings, canederli are a popular dish in the Dolomites made from stale bread, milk, eggs, and a variety of fillings such as speck, cheese, or vegetables. These hearty dumplings are typically boiled and served in broth or with a rich sauce for a comforting meal.

3. Polenta: A staple of northern Italian cuisine, polenta is a cornmeal-based dish that is often served as a side dish or main course in the Dolomites. This creamy and hearty dish can be paired with a variety of toppings such as mushrooms, cheese, or sausages for a satisfying meal.

4. Goulash: Influenced by neighboring Austria and Hungary, goulash is a popular dish in the Dolomites that consists of tender chunks of beef stewed with onions, paprika, and other spices until rich and flavorful. This warming dish is often served with polenta or bread for a filling and delicious meal.

5. Strudel: A classic dessert in the Dolomites, strudel is a flaky pastry filled with apples, raisins, nuts, and cinnamon that is baked until golden and crispy. This sweet treat is often

served warm with a dollop of whipped cream or vanilla sauce for a delightful end to a meal.

6. Bombardino: A popular après-ski drink in the Dolomites, the Bombardino is a creamy and indulgent cocktail made from equal parts eggnog and brandy topped with whipped cream. Served hot, this comforting drink is perfect for warming up after a day on the slopes.

7. Vin Brulè: Also known as mulled wine, Vin Brulè is a spiced and heated wine that is popular during the winter months in the Dolomites. Made with red wine, sugar, cinnamon, cloves, and citrus peel, this aromatic drink is perfect for sipping by the fire after a day of outdoor activities.

8. Grappa: A strong and aromatic spirit made from distilling grape pomace, grappa is a traditional digestif in the Dolomites that is often enjoyed after a meal to aid digestion. This potent drink comes in a variety of flavors and strengths, making it a favorite among locals and visitors alike.

From savory meats to sweet desserts and warming drinks, the Dolomites offer a diverse range of flavors that highlight the region's culinary traditions. Whether you're exploring mountain huts or dining in gourmet restaurants, be sure to sample these must-try local dishes and drinks for an authentic taste of the Dolomites.

Best Shopping Spots in the Dolomites

The Dolomites, with their stunning alpine landscapes and charming mountain villages, offer a unique shopping experience that combines traditional craftsmanship with modern design. From local artisans selling handmade goods to upscale boutiques featuring high-end fashion, there is something for every shopper in this picturesque region. Here are some of the best shopping spots in the Dolomites, complete with addresses and phone numbers for your convenience:

1. Ortisei: Located in the Val Gardena valley, Ortisei is known for its woodcarving tradition and artisanal craftsmanship. The pedestrianized town center is lined with shops selling intricately carved wooden sculptures, furniture, and souvenirs. Visit La Stua Boutique (Str. Rezia, 73, 39046

Ortisei) for a selection of high-quality wooden products and home decor items. Phone: +39 0471 796034.

2. Cortina d'Ampezzo: As one of the most glamorous ski resorts in the Dolomites, Cortina d'Ampezzo boasts a range of upscale boutiques and designer stores. Stroll along Corso Italia, the main shopping street, to find luxury fashion brands, jewelry stores, and specialty shops. Stop by Luis Trenker (Corso Italia, 60, 32043 Cortina d'Ampezzo) for stylish alpine-inspired clothing and accessories. Phone: +39 0436 868045.

3. Brunico: This charming town in the Pusteria valley is home to a mix of traditional shops and modern boutiques. Explore the historic center to discover local products such as wool textiles, ceramics, and leather goods. Don't miss a visit to Sport Mode Alpin (Via Bastioni, 8, 39031 Brunico) for a selection of outdoor clothing and gear. Phone: +39 0474 553481.

4. Bolzano: The capital of South Tyrol, Bolzano offers a vibrant shopping scene with a mix of international brands and local artisans. Wander through the medieval streets of the old

town to find specialty food shops, wine cellars, and boutiques selling handmade goods. Visit Römerpassage (Via Museo, 25, 39100 Bolzano) for a range of fashion and lifestyle stores under one roof. Phone: +39 0471 980999.

5. Merano: Known for its spa culture and lush gardens, Merano also offers a variety of shopping opportunities. Explore the elegant arcades of the old town to find boutique stores selling clothing, accessories, and home decor items. Make sure to visit Galleria Merano (Corso Libertà, 45, 39012 Merano) for a curated selection of designer fashion brands. Phone: +39 0473 232350.

6. Bressanone: Nestled in the Isarco valley, Bressanone is a picturesque town with a rich history of craftsmanship. Stroll through the cobbled streets to discover artisan workshops selling ceramics, glassware, and handmade jewelry. Head to Boutique Hanny (Via Cappuccini, 18, 39042 Bressanone) for a collection of elegant women's clothing and accessories. Phone: +39 0472 832088.

7. San Candido: This charming village in the Alta Pusteria valley is a hidden gem for shopping enthusiasts. Browse the

local shops to find handmade lace products, wooden toys, and gourmet food items. Stop by Boutique Tschurtschenthaler (Via dei Tintori, 1, 39038 San Candido) for a selection of high-quality fashion brands and accessories. Phone: +39 0474 913280.

8. Selva di Val Gardena: Situated at the foot of the Sella massif, Selva di Val Gardena is a hub for outdoor enthusiasts and art lovers alike. Explore the town's galleries and craft shops to find unique souvenirs and gifts made by local artists. Visit Artigianato Val Gardena (Str. Meisules, 213/A, 39048 Selva di Val Gardena) for a range of handcrafted wooden products and decorative items. Phone: +39 0471 795352.

Whether you're looking for traditional handicrafts, designer fashion, or gourmet treats, the Dolomites offer a diverse shopping experience that reflects the region's rich cultural heritage and natural beauty. Take some time to explore these top shopping spots during your visit to the Dolomites and bring home a piece of this enchanting alpine paradise.

CHAPTER 5

ACCOMMODATION AND
SCENIC SPOTS

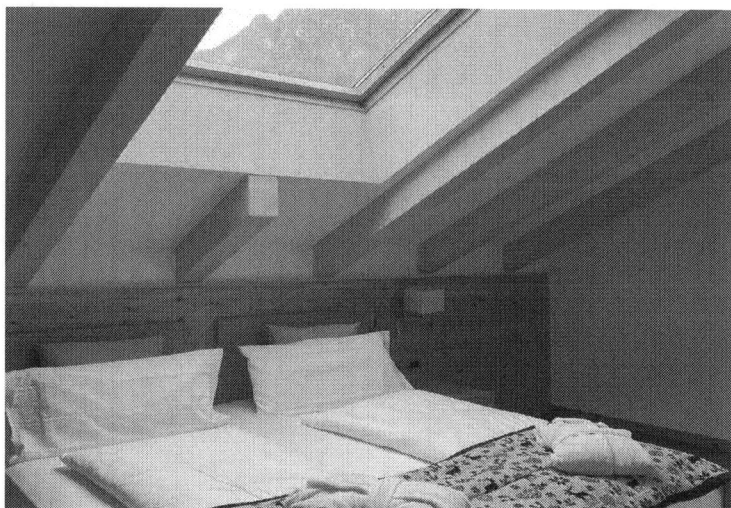

Where to Stay in the Dolomites

Dolomites have something for everyone. Here are some of the best places to stay in this stunning region, complete with descriptions and contact information for your convenience:

1. Luxury Resorts

Rosa Alpina Hotel & Spa (Strada Micurà de Rü, 20, 39030 San Cassiano): Nestled in the heart of the Alta Badia region, this five-star hotel offers luxurious accommodations, gourmet dining, and a world-class spa. Enjoy stunning views of the surrounding mountains from your elegant room or suite, and indulge in pampering treatments at the on-site wellness center. Phone: +39 0471 849500.

Adler Mountain Lodge (St. Zyprianweg, 17, 39050 Alpe di Siusi): Located on the Alpe di Siusi plateau, this exclusive mountain retreat combines rustic charm with modern amenities. Stay in a cozy chalet with panoramic views of the Dolomites, and savor delicious regional cuisine at the lodge's restaurant. Relax in the outdoor infinity pool or unwind in the sauna after a day of hiking or skiing. Phone: +39 0471 723000.

2. Boutique Hotels

Hotel La Perla (Strada Micurà de Rü, 48, 39030 Corvara): Situated in the picturesque village of Corvara, this boutique hotel offers stylish accommodations and personalized service.

Each room is elegantly furnished with local materials and features modern amenities such as a private balcony and free Wi-Fi. Enjoy gourmet meals at the hotel's Michelin-starred restaurant and relax in the wellness area with a sauna and steam bath. Phone: +39 0471 831000.

Hotel Laurin (Via Laurin, 4, 39042 Bressanone): Located in the historic center of Bressanone, this charming hotel combines traditional Tyrolean architecture with contemporary design. The cozy rooms are decorated in warm colors and feature wooden furniture, plush bedding, and mountain views. Start your day with a hearty breakfast buffet and explore the town's shops and attractions just steps away from the hotel. Phone: +39 0472 830200.

3. Mountain Huts

Rifugio Lagazuoi (Località Passo Falzarego, 32043 Cortina d'Ampezzo): Perched at an altitude of 2,752 meters on Mount Lagazuoi, this mountain hut offers cozy dormitory-style accommodations with stunning views of the surrounding peaks. Accessible by cable car or hiking trail, the rifugio is a popular base for hikers and climbers exploring the area. Enjoy hearty meals made with local ingredients at the on-site restaurant and soak up the panoramic vistas from the terrace. Phone: +39 0436 867303.

Rifugio Fanes (Località Pederü, 32040 San Vigilio di Marebbe): Tucked away in the Fanes-Sennes-Braies Nature Park, this rustic mountain hut provides simple yet comfortable rooms and dormitories for hikers and nature lovers. Surrounded by meadows and forests, the rifugio offers a peaceful retreat from the hustle and bustle of everyday life. Enjoy traditional South Tyrolean dishes at the cozy restaurant and explore the nearby hiking trails leading to scenic viewpoints. Phone: +39 0474 501086.

4. Family-Friendly Hotels

Family Hotel Biancaneve (Strada Plan de Corones, 10, 39030 San Vigilio di Marebbe): Ideal for families with children, this welcoming hotel in San Vigilio di Marebbe offers spacious rooms, a kids' club, and a variety of indoor and outdoor activities for all ages. Parents can relax in the spa area while kids have fun at the playroom or outdoor playground. The hotel's restaurant serves delicious meals made with fresh local ingredients. Phone: +39 0474 501043.

Hotel Adler (Via Rezia, 7, 39030 Ortisei): Located in the charming village of Ortisei, this family-friendly hotel features comfortable rooms, a heated outdoor pool, and a children's play area. The hotel offers special amenities for families such as baby equipment rental, kids' menus, and organized activities for children. Parents can unwind in the sauna or enjoy a massage at the spa while kids have fun at the supervised kids' club. Phone: +39 0471 796033.

5. Agriturismos

Agriturismo Maso Plaz (Via Plazores, 10, 38035 Moena): Set on a working farm in the Val di Fassa valley, this agriturismo offers cozy apartments with traditional furnishings and modern amenities. Guests can participate in farm activities such as milking cows, collecting eggs, and harvesting fruits and vegetables. Enjoy homemade meals prepared with farm-fresh ingredients at the on-site restaurant and explore the scenic surroundings on hiking or biking trails. Phone: +39 0462 573277.

Agriturismo Maso Corradini (Via Corradini, 8/A, 39040 Castelrotto): Surrounded by vineyards and apple orchards in the Alpe di Siusi region, this charming agriturismo provides comfortable rooms and apartments with panoramic views of the Dolomites. Guests can taste local wines and homemade products at the farm's tasting room or join guided tours of the property to learn about sustainable farming practices. Relax in the garden or explore nearby villages on foot or by bike. Phone: +39 0471 705091.

Whether you're seeking luxury accommodations, boutique hotels, mountain huts, family-friendly resorts, or agriturismos, the Dolomites offer a diverse range of lodging options to suit every traveler's needs. Choose one of these top places to stay during your visit to this enchanting alpine paradise and make your stay in the Dolomites truly unforgettable.

Best Scenic Spots in the Dolomites

The Dolomites, a UNESCO World Heritage Site located in northeastern Italy, are renowned for their stunning mountain landscapes, dramatic rock formations, and picturesque alpine villages. This breathtaking region offers a plethora of scenic spots that showcase the natural beauty and unique geology of the Dolomites. From towering peaks and crystal-clear lakes to lush valleys and charming meadows, here are some of the best scenic spots in the Dolomites that are sure to leave you in awe:

1. Tre Cime di Lavaredo

One of the most iconic landmarks in the Dolomites, the Tre Cime di Lavaredo (Three Peaks of Lavaredo) is a trio of distinctive peaks that dominate the skyline. Located in the Sexten Dolomites, these towering rock formations are a favorite among hikers, climbers, and photographers. The best vantage point to admire the Tre Cime is from the Rifugio Auronzo, where you can enjoy panoramic views of these majestic peaks against the backdrop of the surrounding mountains.

2. Lago di Braies

Nestled in the heart of the Fanes-Sennes-Braies Nature Park, Lago di Braies (Lake Braies) is a crystal-clear alpine lake surrounded by lush forests and towering peaks. The emerald waters of the lake reflect the dramatic cliffs and pine forests, creating a picture-perfect setting for nature lovers and photographers. Take a leisurely stroll around the lake, rent a rowboat to explore its tranquil waters, or hike to higher viewpoints for breathtaking vistas of this idyllic spot.

3. Seceda

Located above the charming village of Ortisei in Val Gardena, Seceda is a stunning plateau with sweeping views of the surrounding Dolomite peaks. Accessible by cable car from Ortisei or by hiking trails, Seceda offers panoramic vistas of the Odle Group and Puez-Odle Nature Park. The rolling meadows dotted with wildflowers, rugged cliffs, and distant mountain ranges make Seceda a popular spot for hikers, photographers, and nature enthusiasts seeking solitude and serenity.

4. Passo Giau

Situated at an altitude of 2,236 meters, Passo Giau is a mountain pass that offers breathtaking views of the surrounding peaks and valleys. Located between Cortina d'Ampezzo and Colle Santa Lucia, Passo Giau is a popular stop for cyclists, motorcyclists, and hikers exploring the Dolomites. The panoramic drive along winding roads lined with wildflowers and rugged cliffs provides ample opportunities to capture the beauty of this alpine landscape.

5. Alpe di Siusi

The Alpe di Siusi (Seiser Alm) is Europe's largest alpine plateau, located in the heart of the Dolomites near the villages of Castelrotto and Ortisei. This vast expanse of meadows, forests, and rolling hills offers stunning views of the surrounding peaks, including the Langkofel and Plattkofel mountains. Hike or bike along scenic trails, enjoy traditional South Tyrolean cuisine at rustic mountain huts, or simply relax amidst the natural beauty of this enchanting alpine paradise.

6. Val di Funes

Tucked away in a secluded valley near the town of Santa Maddalena, Val di Funes (Villnößtal) is a hidden gem in the Dolomites known for its postcard-perfect landscapes and charming hamlets. The valley is framed by the jagged peaks of the Geisler Group, which provide a dramatic backdrop for lush meadows, rustic farmhouses, and historic churches. Explore hiking trails that wind through flower-filled meadows, visit traditional alpine villages, or simply soak in the tranquility of this pristine valley.

7. Cinque Torri

Located near Cortina d'Ampezzo, the Cinque Torri (Five Towers) are a group of striking rock formations that have become a popular destination for climbers and hikers. These distinctive towers rise dramatically from the surrounding meadows and forests, offering a unique backdrop for outdoor adventures. Take a leisurely stroll around the base of the towers, hike to higher viewpoints for panoramic vistas, or simply marvel at the geological wonders of this captivating landscape.

8. Lake Misurina

Situated at an altitude of 1,754 meters near Cortina d'Ampezzo, Lake Misurina is a picturesque alpine lake surrounded by lush forests and towering peaks. The tranquil waters of the lake reflect the majestic peaks of the Cadini di Misurina range, creating a stunning backdrop for outdoor activities such as hiking, boating, and picnicking. Enjoy panoramic views of the lake and surrounding mountains from scenic viewpoints along its shores or explore nearby hiking trails that lead to hidden waterfalls and panoramic vistas.

9. Val Gardena

Val Gardena (Gröden) is a picturesque valley nestled between the towering peaks of the Dolomites, renowned for its natural beauty and charming villages. The valley is home to popular resorts such as Ortisei, Selva di Val Gardena, and Santa Cristina, each offering stunning views of the surrounding mountains and access to a wide range of outdoor activities. Explore hiking trails that wind through lush forests and alpine meadows, visit traditional wood-carving workshops in quaint villages, or simply relax amidst the serene beauty of this enchanting valley.

10. Sella Pass

Connecting Val Gardena with Alta Badia and Val di Fassa, Sella Pass is a scenic mountain pass that offers panoramic views of some of the most iconic peaks in the Dolomites. The winding road through Sella Pass provides breathtaking vistas of rugged cliffs, lush valleys, and snow-capped peaks at every turn. Stop at scenic overlooks to capture the beauty of this alpine landscape or embark on hikes that lead to hidden lakes and majestic viewpoints.

The Dolomites are home to some of the most spectacular scenic spots in Europe, each offering a unique perspective on this enchanting alpine paradise. Whether you're seeking panoramic vistas of towering peaks, tranquil lakes surrounded by lush forests, or charming valleys dotted with picturesque villages, the Dolomites have something to offer every nature lover and outdoor enthusiast. Explore these top scenic spots in the Dolomites to experience the beauty and majesty of this UNESCO World Heritage Site firsthand and create unforgettable memories in one of Italy's most captivating regions.

Best Luxury Hotels in the Dolomites

The Dolomites, a UNESCO World Heritage Site in northeastern Italy, are not only known for their stunning natural beauty and outdoor adventures but also for their luxurious accommodations that offer unparalleled comfort and hospitality. From elegant mountain lodges to exclusive alpine retreats, the Dolomites boast a range of luxury hotels that cater to discerning travelers seeking a lavish getaway in this picturesque region. Whether you're looking for a romantic escape, a wellness retreat, or a gourmet experience, these top luxury hotels in the Dolomites are sure to exceed your expectations and provide an unforgettable stay amidst the breathtaking mountain landscapes.

1. Rosa Alpina Hotel & Spa

Nestled in the charming village of San Cassiano in Alta Badia, Rosa Alpina Hotel & Spa is a five-star luxury hotel renowned for its refined elegance and warm hospitality. This family-run hotel combines traditional alpine charm with modern amenities, offering luxurious rooms and suites with stunning mountain views, gourmet dining experiences at the Michelin-starred restaurant St. Hubertus, and a world-class spa with holistic wellness treatments. Guests can enjoy personalized service, outdoor activities such as hiking and skiing, and exclusive access to the hotel's private chalet for a truly indulgent mountain retreat.

2. Lefay Resort & SPA Dolomiti

Located in the picturesque town of Pinzolo in the Adamello Brenta Nature Park, Lefay Resort & SPA Dolomiti is a luxurious eco-friendly resort that blends contemporary design with sustainable practices. Surrounded by lush forests and majestic peaks, this five-star resort offers elegant suites and residences with panoramic views, a state-of-the-art spa with wellness programs inspired by nature, and gourmet dining featuring organic and locally sourced ingredients. Guests can unwind in the infinity pools overlooking the Dolomites, participate in outdoor activities like yoga and hiking, and experience the ultimate relaxation in a serene mountain setting.

3. Hotel Sassongher

Perched on a hilltop overlooking the charming village of Corvara in Alta Badia, Hotel Sassongher is a five-star luxury hotel that exudes Tyrolean charm and sophistication. This exclusive hotel features spacious rooms and suites with alpine-inspired décor, a gourmet restaurant serving regional specialties and international cuisine, and a wellness center with indoor and outdoor pools, saunas, and holistic treatments. Guests can enjoy personalized service, access to the hotel's private ski shuttle to the nearby slopes, and stunning views of the Sella Group and Puez-Odle Nature Park from the hotel's panoramic terrace.

4. Alpina Dolomites Gardena Health Lodge & Spa

Situated in the scenic Val Gardena valley near the village of Selva di Val Gardena, Alpina Dolomites Gardena Health

Lodge & Spa is a luxury wellness retreat that offers a harmonious blend of relaxation and rejuvenation. This five-star hotel features elegant rooms and suites with modern amenities and alpine accents, a gourmet restaurant showcasing local and organic cuisine, and a state-of-the-art spa with thermal pools, saunas, and holistic treatments. Guests can unwind in the tranquil garden, participate in yoga and meditation sessions, and explore the surrounding mountains on guided hikes or bike tours for a truly immersive wellness experience.

5. Cristallo, a Luxury Collection Resort & Spa

Located in the prestigious resort town of Cortina d'Ampezzo, Cristallo, a Luxury Collection Resort & Spa is an iconic five-star hotel that epitomizes luxury and sophistication in the heart of the Dolomites. This historic hotel boasts elegant rooms and suites with classic décor and modern amenities, multiple dining options ranging from gourmet cuisine to casual fare, and an exclusive spa offering bespoke wellness treatments and relaxation experiences. Guests can enjoy personalized concierge service, access to private ski slopes, and panoramic views of the Dolomite peaks from the hotel's terrace while savoring the timeless elegance of this legendary alpine retreat.

6. Adler Mountain Lodge

Perched on a sunny plateau overlooking the stunning Alpe di Siusi in the Sciliar-Catinaccio Nature Park, Adler Mountain Lodge is a luxurious eco-friendly retreat that offers a unique blend of alpine charm and contemporary design. This five-star lodge features spacious chalets with panoramic views of the Dolomites, gourmet dining showcasing local flavors and international cuisine, and a wellness center with indoor and outdoor pools, saunas, and holistic treatments inspired by nature. Guests can unwind in the tranquility of the mountains, participate in outdoor activities such as hiking and skiing, and experience the ultimate relaxation amidst the pristine beauty of this exclusive alpine sanctuary.

The Dolomites are home to some of the best luxury hotels in Europe that cater to travelers seeking an upscale mountain retreat amidst breathtaking natural landscapes. Whether you're looking for a romantic escape, a wellness getaway, or a gourmet experience, these top luxury hotels in the Dolomites offer impeccable service, elegant accommodations, and world-class amenities that promise an unforgettable stay in this enchanting alpine paradise. Indulge in the opulence of these exclusive mountain retreats and immerse yourself in the beauty and tranquility of the Dolomites for a truly luxurious experience that will leave you rejuvenated and inspired.

Best Budget-Friendly Accommodations in the Dolomites

The Dolomites, a UNESCO World Heritage Site in northeastern Italy, are not only known for their stunning natural beauty and luxurious accommodations but also for their budget-friendly options that cater to travelers seeking affordable yet comfortable stays in this picturesque region. From cozy mountain lodges to family-run guesthouses, the Dolomites offer a range of budget-friendly accommodations that provide a welcoming atmosphere and convenient amenities without breaking the bank. Whether you're a solo traveler on a tight budget, a couple looking for a cozy retreat, or a family seeking affordable options, these best budget-friendly accommodations in the Dolomites are sure to offer a memorable stay amidst the breathtaking mountain landscapes.

1. Rifugio Alpe di Tires

Located in the heart of the Alpe di Siusi plateau, Rifugio Alpe di Tires is a charming mountain hut that offers budget-friendly accommodation for hikers, nature lovers, and outdoor enthusiasts. This rustic lodge features simple yet comfortable rooms with shared bathrooms, a cozy dining area serving traditional South Tyrolean cuisine, and a sunny terrace with panoramic views of the surrounding mountains. Guests can enjoy hiking trails right at their doorstep, participate in guided excursions, and experience the tranquility of the alpine meadows while staying within budget-friendly rates.

2. Hotel Lupo Bianco

Situated in the scenic Val di Fassa valley near the village of Canazei, Hotel Lupo Bianco is a family-run hotel that provides affordable accommodation with a warm and welcoming atmosphere. This cozy hotel offers comfortable rooms with modern amenities, a hearty breakfast buffet to start the day, and a traditional restaurant serving regional specialties and Italian classics. Guests can relax in the garden, explore the nearby hiking and biking trails, and enjoy easy access to the ski slopes in winter for a budget-friendly mountain getaway in the Dolomites.

3. Garni Aritz

Located in the charming town of Campitello di Fassa in Val di Fassa valley, Garni Aritz is a budget-friendly bed and breakfast that offers cozy accommodation and personalized service for guests looking for a comfortable stay at affordable rates. This family-friendly guesthouse features well-appointed rooms with mountain views, a generous breakfast buffet to fuel your adventures, and a wellness area with sauna and Turkish bath for relaxation after a day of exploring the Dolomites. Guests can take advantage of the hotel's central location, close to restaurants, shops, and outdoor activities, making it an ideal base for budget-conscious travelers.

4. Hotel Cesa Padon

Nestled in the picturesque village of Rocca Pietore near the Marmolada glacier, Hotel Cesa Padon is a budget-friendly hotel that offers simple yet comfortable accommodation with a focus on hospitality and affordability. This family-run hotel features cozy rooms with traditional décor, a restaurant serving homemade dishes and local specialties, and a friendly staff who are eager to help guests make the most of their stay in the Dolomites. Guests can explore nearby hiking trails, visit historic sites like the Serrai di Sottoguda canyon, and enjoy the peaceful ambiance of this charming mountain retreat without breaking the bank.

5. Garni Settsass

Situated in the scenic village of Selva di Cadore in the heart of the Dolomites, Garni Settsass is a budget-friendly guesthouse that offers comfortable accommodation and personalized service for travelers seeking an affordable mountain retreat. This cozy bed and breakfast features spacious rooms with modern amenities, a generous breakfast buffet with homemade pastries and local products, and a welcoming atmosphere that makes guests feel at home during their stay. Guests can explore the nearby hiking trails, visit historic landmarks like the Museo Vittorino Cazzetta, and experience the beauty of the Dolomites without compromising on comfort or budget.

Whether you're looking for a simple mountain hut experience, a cozy bed and breakfast, or a family-run hotel with personalized service, these best budget-friendly accommodations in the Dolomites provide comfort, convenience, and affordability without sacrificing the charm and beauty of this UNESCO World Heritage Site. Enjoy a memorable stay amidst the breathtaking mountain landscapes of the Dolomites while staying within your budget and experiencing the warmth and hospitality of these affordable mountain retreats.

Recommended Dolomites Hotels

From luxurious resorts to cozy mountain lodges, there is something for everyone in this stunning alpine region. In this guide, we will explore some of the recommended hotels in the Dolomites, including their opening hours, admission fees (if applicable), contact information, address, and phone numbers.

1. Hotel Adler Spa Resort Dolomiti
   - Opening Hours: The hotel is open year-round.
   - Admission Fee: Rates vary depending on the season and room type.
   - Contact: info@dolomiti.it
   - Address: Strada Rezia 7, 39030 Ortisei, Italy
   - Phone Number: +39 0471 775000

Hotel Adler Spa Resort Dolomiti is a luxurious five-star hotel located in Ortisei, a charming town in Val Gardena. This elegant resort offers spacious rooms and suites with stunning mountain views, a world-class spa with indoor and outdoor pools, and gourmet dining options. Guests can enjoy a range of activities, from skiing in winter to hiking and biking in summer. The hotel's attentive staff ensures a memorable stay for all guests.

2. Rifugio Lagazuoi

- Opening Hours: The rifugio is open during the summer and winter seasons.
- Admission Fee: Prices vary for accommodation and meals.
- Contact: info@rifugiolagazuoi.com
- Address: Passo Falzarego, 32043 Cortina d'Ampezzo BL, Italy
- Phone Number: +39 0436 867303

Rifugio Lagazuoi is a mountain refuge located at an altitude of 2,752 meters on Mount Lagazuoi. This unique accommodation offers dormitory-style rooms and private bedrooms with shared bathrooms. Guests can enjoy traditional Italian cuisine at the rifugio's restaurant while taking in panoramic views of the Dolomites. The rifugio is accessible by cable car or hiking trails and is a popular stop for hikers and climbers.

3. Hotel La Perla

- Opening Hours: The hotel is open year-round.
- Admission Fee: Rates vary depending on the season and room type.
- Contact: info@hotellaperla.net
- Address: Strada Col Alt 105, 39033 Corvara in Badia BZ, Italy
- Phone Number: +39 0471 831000

Hotel La Perla is a luxury hotel located in Corvara, a picturesque village in Alta Badia. This five-star property features elegantly appointed rooms and suites, a Michelin-starred restaurant, and a spa with a range of wellness treatments. Guests can participate in guided hikes, mountain biking excursions, and skiing adventures during the winter months. The hotel's attentive staff ensures a personalized and memorable experience for all guests.

4. Rifugio Fanes:

- Opening Hours: The rifugio is open during the summer season.
- Admission Fee: Prices vary for accommodation and meals.
- Contact: info@rifugiofanes.com
- Address: Strada de Fanes 17, 39030 San Vigilio di Marebbe BZ, Italy
- Phone Number: +39 0474 501212

Rifugio Fanes is a mountain hut located in the Fanes-Senes-Braies Nature Park near San Vigilio di Marebbe. This rustic accommodation offers dormitory-style rooms and traditional South Tyrolean cuisine at its restaurant. Guests can explore the surrounding hiking trails and enjoy the tranquility of the alpine meadows. The rifugio is accessible by foot or by shuttle bus from the village.

5. Hotel Tyrol

- Opening Hours: The hotel is open year-round.
- Admission Fee: Rates vary depending on the season and room type.
- Contact: info@hoteltyrol.info

- Address: Strada Rezia 9, 39030 Selva di Val Gardena BZ, Italy
- Phone Number: +39 0471 795136

Hotel Tyrol is a family-run hotel located in Selva di Val Gardena, a popular ski resort town in the Dolomites. This charming hotel offers comfortable rooms, a wellness center with saunas and steam baths, and a restaurant serving traditional Tyrolean cuisine. Guests can take ad

vantage of the hotel's central location for easy access to ski slopes in winter and hiking trails in summer. The hotel's friendly staff ensures a warm and welcoming atmosphere for all guests.

The Dolomites offer a diverse selection of hotels to suit every traveler's preferences and budget. Whether you're looking for a luxurious retreat or a cozy mountain refuge, these recommended hotels in the Dolomites provide comfort, convenience, and personalized service for an unforgettable stay amidst the stunning alpine landscapes. Be sure to check the opening hours, admission fees (if applicable), contact information, address, and phone numbers before booking your accommodation to ensure a smooth and enjoyable experience in this UNESCO World Heritage Site.

CHAPTER 6

DAY TRIPS IN THE
DOLOMITES

Itinerary for a 7-Day Trip to the Dolomites

A 7-day trip to the Dolomites offers a perfect balance of adventure, relaxation, and cultural exploration in one of the most stunning alpine regions in the world. With its jagged peaks, lush valleys, and charming villages, the Dolomites provide a diverse array of activities and experiences for travelers of all interests. In this detailed itinerary, we will outline a week-long journey through the Dolomites, highlighting the best sights, activities, and accommodations along the way.

Day 1: Arrival in Bolzano
- Arrive in Bolzano, the capital of South Tyrol, and check into your hotel.
- Explore the historic city center, visit the South Tyrol Museum of Archaeology to see Ötzi the Iceman, and stroll through the charming streets lined with medieval buildings.
- Enjoy a traditional South Tyrolean dinner at a local restaurant and sample regional specialties like speck, knödel, and strudel.

Accommodation: Hotel Greif (Address: Piazza Walther 1, 39100 Bolzano BZ, Italy; Phone: +39 0471 318000)

Day 2: Seiser Alm and Alpe di Siusi
- Take a scenic drive to Seiser Alm, Europe's largest alpine plateau, and explore the picturesque meadows and forests.

- Hike or bike along the well-marked trails, enjoy panoramic views of the surrounding mountains, and spot wildlife such as marmots and chamois.
- Visit the village of Compatsch for lunch and try local dishes at a mountain hut.

Accommodation: Seiser Alm Urthaler (Address: Seiser Alm 30, 39040 Alpe di Siusi BZ, Italy; Phone: +39 0471 727927)

Day 3: Val Gardena
- Drive to Val Gardena, a valley known for its charming villages, world-class skiing, and stunning mountain scenery.
- Take a cable car ride to Seceda for breathtaking views of the Dolomites, go for a hike in the Puez-Odle Nature Park, or visit the Museum Gherdëina in Ortisei to learn about local history and culture.
- Relax in the afternoon at your hotel's spa or explore the shops and cafes in the village.

Accommodation: Hotel Adler Spa Resort Dolomiti (Address: Strada Rezia 7, 39030 Ortisei BZ, Italy; Phone: +39 0471 775000)

Day 4: Alta Badia

- Head to Alta Badia, a region known for its gourmet cuisine, scenic beauty, and outdoor activities.
- Visit the village of Corvara and take a guided hike or e-bike tour to explore the surrounding mountains and valleys.
- Enjoy a leisurely lunch at a mountain hut or Michelin-starred restaurant, then relax at your hotel's wellness center.

Accommodation: Hotel La Perla (Address: Strada Col Alt 105, 39033 Corvara in Badia BZ, Italy; Phone: +39 0471 831000)

Day 5: Cortina d'Ampezzo

- Drive to Cortina d'Ampezzo, a chic resort town surrounded by towering peaks and lush forests.
- Explore the town's boutiques, cafes, and art galleries, visit the Olympic Ice Stadium and Museo Paleontologico "Rinaldo Zardini," or take a scenic drive along the Great Dolomite Road.
- In the evening, dine at a local restaurant and savor traditional Venetian dishes.

Accommodation: Hotel de la Poste (Address: Piazza Roma 14, 32043 Cortina d'Ampezzo BL, Italy; Phone: +39 0436 4221)

Day 6: Tre Cime di Lavaredo
- Embark on a day trip to Tre Cime di Lavaredo, one of the most iconic landmarks in the Dolomites.
- Hike the classic Tre Cime loop trail for stunning views of the three distinctive peaks, explore World War I tunnels and trenches along the way, and enjoy a picnic lunch amidst the dramatic scenery.
- Return to your hotel in Cortina d'Ampezzo for a relaxing evening and farewell dinner.

Accommodation: Hotel de la Poste (Address: Piazza Roma 14, 32043 Cortina d'Ampezzo BL, Italy; Phone: +39 0436 4221)

Day 7: Departure from Bolzano
- Check out of your hotel in Cortina d'Ampezzo and drive back to Bolzano for your departure.

- If time allows, visit a local winery in South Tyrol for a wine tasting experience or stop at Lake Carezza for a final glimpse of the Dolomites' beauty.
- Depart from Bolzano with unforgettable memories of your week-long adventure in the Dolomites.

CHAPTER 7

MAKING THE MOST OF YOUR MONEY AND OUTDOOR ACTIVITIES

Money-Saving Tips for Traveling in the Dolomites

Traveling in the Dolomites, a stunning mountain range in Italy, can be a dream come true for outdoor enthusiasts and nature lovers. However, exploring this picturesque region can sometimes come with a hefty price tag. To help you make the most of your trip without breaking the bank, here are some money-saving tips to keep in mind:

1. Travel Off-Peak: Consider visiting the Dolomites during the shoulder seasons, such as spring or fall, to take advantage of lower accommodation prices and fewer crowds. Additionally, airfares and car rental rates tend to be more affordable during these times.

2. Book Accommodation in Advance: To secure the best deals on accommodation, make sure to book well in advance. Look for budget-friendly options such as hostels, guesthouses, or self-catering apartments to save on lodging costs.

3. Pack Your Own Food: Eating out every meal can quickly add up, so consider packing some snacks and simple meals to enjoy while you're out exploring the Dolomites. This can help you save money on dining expenses and allow you to splurge on a few special meals.

4. Use Public Transportation: Instead of renting a car, consider using public transportation to get around the

Dolomites. The region is well-connected by buses and trains, making it easy to explore the area without the added expense of a rental car.

5. Take Advantage of Free Activities: Enjoy the natural beauty of the Dolomites without spending a dime by taking advantage of free activities such as hiking, cycling, or simply taking in the breathtaking views. Many trails and viewpoints are easily accessible and offer a budget-friendly way to experience the beauty of the region.

6. Look for Discount Passes: Consider purchasing a regional pass or discount card that offers savings on attractions, transportation, and other activities in the Dolomites. These passes can help you save money while still enjoying all that the region has to offer.

7. Shop at Local Markets: Save money on groceries and souvenirs by shopping at local markets and stores in the Dolomites. You'll find fresh produce, local products, and unique gifts at more affordable prices than touristy shops and restaurants.

8. Stay in Mountain Huts: For a unique and budget-friendly accommodation option, consider staying in mountain huts or rifugios while hiking in the Dolomites. These rustic lodgings offer basic amenities and stunning views at a fraction of the cost of traditional hotels.

9. Pack Light: Avoid excess baggage fees by packing light for your trip to the Dolomites. Stick to the essentials and versatile clothing items that can be mixed and matched to create different outfits for various activities.

10. Plan Your Itinerary Wisely: To make the most of your time in the Dolomites without overspending, plan your itinerary wisely. Research free or low-cost activities, prioritize must-see sights, and leave room for spontaneous adventures to make the most of your budget.

By following these money-saving tips, you can enjoy a memorable and budget-friendly trip to the Dolomites without sacrificing the beauty and adventure that this stunning region has to offer. Happy travels!

Insider Tips for Exploring the Dolomites

Dolomites offer a wealth of opportunities for exploration and discovery. To make the most of your visit to this stunning mountain range, consider these insider tips for exploring the Dolomites:

1. Plan Your Trip in Advance: Before setting off on your Dolomites adventure, take the time to research and plan your trip carefully. Consider factors such as the best time to visit, weather conditions, accommodation options, and must-see attractions. Planning ahead will help you make the most of your time in the region and ensure a smooth and enjoyable experience.

2. Choose the Right Base: When exploring the Dolomites, it's essential to choose the right base for your stay. Consider staying in one of the charming mountain towns or villages such as Cortina d'Ampezzo, Selva di Val Gardena, or Corvara. These bases offer easy access to hiking trails, ski slopes, and other attractions, making them ideal starting points for your adventures in the Dolomites.

3. Get Off the Beaten Path: While popular spots like the Tre Cime di Lavaredo and the Sella Ronda are must-see attractions in the Dolomites, don't be afraid to venture off the beaten path and explore lesser-known areas. Hidden gems like the Alpe di Siusi plateau, the Val di Funes valley, or the Pale di San Martino range offer stunning landscapes and unique experiences away from the crowds.

4. Hike Like a Local: Hiking is one of the best ways to experience the beauty of the Dolomites up close. To hike like a local, consider taking on some of the region's classic trails such as the Alta Via 1 or Alta Via 2 long-distance routes. These multi-day hikes offer breathtaking views, challenging terrain, and a true sense of adventure in the heart of the Dolomites.

5. Sample Local Cuisine: One of the highlights of any trip to the Dolomites is sampling the delicious local cuisine. From hearty mountain dishes like speck (cured ham), canederli (bread dumplings), and polenta to sweet treats like strudel and kaiserschmarrn, there's no shortage of culinary delights to enjoy in the region. Be sure to dine at mountain huts, rifugios,

and traditional restaurants to savor authentic flavors and warm hospitality.

6. Embrace Outdoor Activities: In addition to hiking, the Dolomites offer a wide range of outdoor activities for all ages and interests. Whether you're into rock climbing, mountain biking, paragliding, or skiing, there's something for everyone in this outdoor playground. Try your hand at a new sport or activity to make the most of your time in the Dolomites and create unforgettable memories.

7. Visit Local Museums and Cultural Sites: While the Dolomites are primarily known for their natural beauty and outdoor pursuits, don't overlook the region's rich cultural heritage. Take some time to visit local museums, churches, and historical sites to learn more about the history and traditions of the Dolomites. Highlights include the Messner Mountain Museum, Ladin Museum, and the charming mountain churches scattered throughout the region.

8. Pack Wisely: When exploring the Dolomites, it's essential to pack wisely for varying weather conditions and outdoor activities. Be sure to bring sturdy hiking boots, layers of

clothing for changing temperatures, sun protection, a refillable water bottle, snacks, a map or GPS device, and other essentials for a comfortable and safe adventure in the mountains.

9. Respect Nature and Wildlife: As you explore the Dolomites, remember to respect nature and wildlife by following Leave No Trace principles and local regulations. Stay on designated trails, avoid littering, minimize noise pollution, and observe wildlife from a safe distance to protect the fragile ecosystems of this pristine mountain region.

10. Capture Memories: Last but not least, don't forget to capture memories of your Dolomites adventure through photography or journaling. The stunning landscapes, vibrant colors, and unique experiences you'll encounter in the region are worth preserving for years to come. Take time to appreciate the beauty around you and document your journey in a way that reflects your personal connection to the Dolomites.

By following these insider tips for exploring the Dolomites, you can make the most of your visit to this breathtaking mountain range and create unforgettable experiences that will stay with you long after you've returned home. Whether you're seeking outdoor thrills, cultural discoveries, or simply a peaceful retreat in nature, the Dolomites have something for everyone to enjoy. Happy exploring!

Outdoor Activities in the Dolomites

From hiking and climbing to skiing and mountain biking, the Dolomites offer a wealth of opportunities for adventure seekers and outdoor enthusiasts of all levels. Whether you're a seasoned athlete looking for a challenge or a leisurely traveler seeking to connect with nature, the Dolomites have something for everyone to enjoy. In this guide, we'll explore some of the top outdoor activities in the Dolomites and provide tips for making the most of your adventure in this spectacular mountain range.

Hiking: Hiking is one of the most popular outdoor activities in the Dolomites, thanks to the region's extensive network of well-marked trails that cater to hikers of all abilities. From leisurely strolls through alpine meadows to challenging ascents of rugged peaks, there's a hike for every preference in the Dolomites. Some of the classic hiking routes include the Alta Via 1 and Alta Via 2 long-distance trails, which traverse the region's most iconic landscapes and offer breathtaking views of the surrounding mountains. Be sure to pack plenty of water, snacks, and sturdy hiking boots for a comfortable and safe hiking experience in the Dolomites.

Climbing: With its sheer rock faces, towering spires, and challenging routes, the Dolomites are a paradise for rock climbers from around the world. Whether you're a beginner looking to try your hand at climbing or an experienced climber seeking a new challenge, there are plenty of climbing opportunities in the region. Popular climbing areas include Cinque Torri, Sella Towers, and the Marmolada Glacier, each offering a unique climbing experience against the backdrop of stunning mountain scenery. If you're new to climbing, consider hiring a local guide to help you navigate the terrain and ensure a safe and enjoyable climbing experience in the Dolomites.

Skiing: In the winter months, the Dolomites transform into a winter wonderland with world-class ski resorts and snow-covered slopes that cater to skiers and snowboarders of all levels. From gentle beginner runs to challenging off-piste descents, there's a ski slope for every skill level in the Dolomites. Popular ski resorts like Cortina d'Ampezzo, Alta Badia, and Val Gardena offer a wide range of ski runs, modern lift systems, and cozy mountain huts where you can warm up with a hot drink after a day on the slopes. Don't forget to pack your ski gear, warm clothing, and sunscreen for a memorable skiing experience in the Dolomites.

Mountain Biking: For adrenaline junkies and cycling enthusiasts, mountain biking is a thrilling way to explore the rugged terrain and scenic trails of the Dolomites. The region offers a variety of mountain biking routes that cater to different skill levels, from easy forest trails to challenging singletracks with steep descents and technical obstacles. Popular mountain biking areas include the Sellaronda MTB Tour, Val di Fassa Bike Park, and Alta Badia Bike Area, each offering a unique biking experience amidst stunning alpine landscapes. Rent a mountain bike or bring your own to explore the diverse terrain and epic views of the Dolomites on two wheels.

Paragliding: For a bird's-eye view of the Dolomites' majestic peaks and valleys, consider trying paragliding during your visit to the region. Paragliding is a popular activity in the Dolomites, thanks to its favorable weather conditions, stunning scenery, and experienced local pilots who can guide you on tandem flights or provide instruction for solo flights. Soar high above the mountains, glide through the valleys, and experience the thrill of flying like a bird as you take in panoramic views of the Dolomites from above. Whether you're a first-time flyer or an experienced paraglider, this unforgettable experience will leave you with lasting memories of your time in the Dolomites.

Via Ferrata: For adventurers seeking a unique and exhilarating experience in the Dolomites,

Via Ferrata offers an exciting way to explore the region's rugged cliffs and rocky terrain. Via Ferrata routes consist of steel cables, ladders, and metal rungs that are fixed to the rock face, allowing climbers to traverse exposed sections safely with the help of harnesses and helmets. Popular Via Ferrata routes include Punta Anna in Cortina d'Ampezzo, Tridentina near Val di Fassa, and Tomaselli in Alta Badia, each offering a thrilling mix of climbing, hiking, and scrambling along breathtaking routes with panoramic views. If you're new to Via Ferrata, consider taking a guided tour with a local expert to ensure a safe and enjoyable experience in this adrenaline-pumping activity.

The Dolomites offer a plethora of outdoor activities for adventure seekers and nature lovers alike. Whether you're hiking through alpine meadows, climbing towering peaks, skiing down snow-covered slopes, mountain biking on rugged trails, paragliding above majestic valleys, or traversing Via Ferrata routes along sheer cliffs, there's no shortage of ways to experience the beauty and excitement of this UNESCO World Heritage Site. Be sure to pack accordingly, follow safety guidelines, and immerse yourself in the natural wonders of the Dolomites for an unforgettable outdoor adventure that will leave you inspired and rejuvenated. Happy exploring!

CHAPTER 8

IMMERSING IN DOLOMITE CULTURE AND HERITAGE

Museums and Galleries

These cultural spaces provide a window into the past, present, and future, offering visitors the opportunity to learn, reflect, and be inspired by a diverse range of artifacts, artworks, and exhibitions.

Museums serve as repositories of knowledge and heritage, housing collections of objects that hold historical, artistic, or scientific significance. They often feature curated exhibitions that highlight specific themes, periods, or cultures, allowing visitors to engage with and explore different aspects of human creativity and ingenuity. From ancient artifacts and archaeological finds to contemporary art installations and interactive displays, museums offer a wealth of educational and enriching experiences for people of all ages and backgrounds.

Art galleries, on the other hand, focus primarily on showcasing visual art, including paintings, sculptures, photographs, and other forms of artistic expression. Galleries provide artists with a platform to exhibit their work to the public, fostering appreciation for creativity and artistic innovation. Visitors to art galleries can immerse themselves in a world of aesthetic beauty, emotional depth, and intellectual stimulation, as they engage with the diverse styles, techniques, and themes explored by artists from around the world.

Both museums and galleries play a vital role in preserving cultural heritage and promoting cultural understanding. By collecting, conserving, and displaying objects of historical or artistic significance, these institutions help to safeguard our shared cultural heritage for future generations. Through exhibitions, educational programs, and outreach initiatives, museums and galleries also strive to foster dialogue, promote diversity, and encourage critical thinking among visitors.

In addition to their role as educational and cultural institutions, museums and galleries also contribute to the local economy and tourism industry. They attract visitors from near and far who are eager to explore their collections, attend special events, and participate in educational programs. Museums and galleries often collaborate with local businesses, hotels, and restaurants to create a vibrant cultural ecosystem that benefits the entire community.

One of the key strengths of museums and galleries is their ability to engage with audiences in a variety of ways. Through interactive exhibits, guided tours, workshops, lectures, and special events, these institutions offer visitors multiple entry points to explore and connect with the content on display.

Whether you're a casual visitor looking to admire beautiful artwork or a dedicated scholar seeking in-depth knowledge on a specific subject, museums and galleries cater to a wide range of interests and preferences.

Moreover, museums and galleries are increasingly embracing digital technologies to enhance the visitor experience and reach new audiences. Virtual tours, online exhibitions, interactive apps, and social media platforms allow people to engage with museum collections and artworks from anywhere in the world. These digital initiatives expand access to cultural resources, promote inclusivity, and encourage lifelong learning beyond the physical confines of the museum or gallery space.

Museum and galleries are invaluable cultural institutions that serve as gateways to knowledge, creativity, and inspiration. By preserving our shared heritage, promoting cultural understanding, stimulating dialogue, and fostering community engagement, these institutions play a vital role in enriching our lives and shaping our collective identity. Whether you're exploring ancient artifacts in a museum or admiring contemporary art in a gallery, the experience of engaging with culture and creativity can be transformative and enlightening. Next time you visit a museum or gallery, take a moment to appreciate the stories behind the exhibits, the passion of the

Historical site and landmark

Historical sites and landmarks hold a special place in our collective memory, serving as tangible reminders of the past and connecting us to the stories, events, and people that have shaped our world. These sites are physical manifestations of history, bearing witness to triumphs, tragedies, and transformations that have left an indelible mark on society. From ancient ruins and architectural wonders to battlefields and monuments, historical sites and landmarks provide us with a window into the past, offering insights into the cultures, civilizations, and events that have defined our shared human experience.

One of the most compelling aspects of historical sites and landmarks is their ability to transport us back in time, allowing us to walk in the footsteps of those who came before us. Whether we're exploring the ruins of an ancient civilization or standing in the shadow of a towering monument, these sites evoke a sense of wonder and awe at the achievements and struggles of past generations. By immersing ourselves in the physical spaces where history unfolded, we can gain a deeper appreciation for the complexities of human existence and the enduring impact of our actions.

Historical sites and landmarks also serve as repositories of cultural heritage, preserving traditions, customs, and values that have been passed down through generations. These sites often represent significant milestones in the development of societies, reflecting the beliefs, aspirations, and achievements of the people who built them. By studying these sites, we can learn about the artistic, architectural, and technological innovations of different time periods and gain insights into the social, political, and economic forces that have shaped our world.

Moreover, historical sites and landmarks play a crucial role in fostering a sense of identity and belonging within communities. They serve as symbols of pride and resilience, reminding us of the struggles and sacrifices that have been made to secure our freedoms and rights. By preserving these sites, we honor the memories of those who came before us and ensure that their stories continue to inspire future generations. Historical sites also provide opportunities for reflection and contemplation, inviting us to consider our place in the larger tapestry of history and to reflect on the lessons we can learn from the past.

In addition to their cultural and historical significance, historical sites and landmarks are also important economic assets that contribute to tourism, local development, and job creation. Visitors from around the world are drawn to these sites to learn about history, experience different cultures, and marvel at the architectural wonders of the past. Tourist dollars generated by these visits help support conservation efforts, infrastructure improvements, and community revitalization projects that benefit both residents and visitors alike.

Furthermore, historical sites and landmarks have the power to educate and inspire people of all ages, backgrounds, and interests. Schools, universities, museums, and heritage organizations often use these sites as educational tools to teach students about history, geography, art, architecture, and other subjects. Through guided tours, interpretive exhibits, interactive displays, and hands-on activities, visitors can engage with history in a meaningful and memorable way, deepening their understanding of the past and fostering a lifelong appreciation for cultural heritage.

Historical sites and landmarks are invaluable treasures that enrich our lives, deepen our understanding of the past, and connect us to our shared humanity. Whether we're marveling at the grandeur of a medieval castle, contemplating the ruins of an ancient civilization, or paying tribute at a memorial to fallen heroes, these sites evoke a sense of wonder, reverence, and gratitude for the legacy of those who have come before us. By preserving these sites for future generations, we ensure that their stories continue to inspire, educate, and unite us in our common journey through time. The next time you visit a historical site or landmark, take a moment to pause, reflect, and appreciate the enduring beauty and significance of these living testaments to our shared history.

Traditional Dolomite Music and Dance

Traditional Dolomite music and dance are deeply rooted in the rich cultural heritage of the Dolomite region in northeastern Italy. This mountainous area, known for its stunning landscapes and vibrant communities, has a long history of traditional music and dance that reflects the region's unique identity and spirit. From lively folk tunes to energetic dances, Dolomite music and dance play a central role in local celebrations, festivals, and social gatherings, bringing people together and fostering a sense of community and tradition.

Music has always been an integral part of life in the Dolomite region, with traditional instruments such as the accordion, clarinet, fiddle, and zither forming the backbone of the local music scene. These instruments, often handmade by skilled artisans, produce a distinctive sound that is both melodic and rhythmic, capturing the essence of the Dolomite culture. The music itself is characterized by lively tempos, intricate melodies, and heartfelt lyrics that speak to the joys and sorrows of everyday life in the mountains.

One of the most popular forms of traditional Dolomite music is the polka, a lively dance tune that originated in central Europe and has become a staple of local festivities in the region. The upbeat tempo and infectious rhythm of the polka make it a favorite among dancers of all ages, who gather in town squares, village halls, and mountain meadows to whirl and twirl to the sounds of the accordion and fiddle. The polka is often accompanied by traditional folk songs that tell stories of love, nature, and daily life in the Dolomites, adding a lyrical dimension to the spirited dance.

In addition to the polka, other traditional dances are also popular in the Dolomite region, each with its own unique steps, movements, and costumes. The schottische, waltz, mazurka, and tarantella are just a few examples of dances that are performed at weddings, festivals, and other special occasions throughout the year. These dances are often passed down from generation to generation, with families and communities coming together to preserve and celebrate their cultural heritage through music and movement.

Traditional Dolomite music and dance are not only forms of entertainment but also expressions of identity, pride, and solidarity among the people of the region. Through music and dance, individuals can connect with their roots, honor their ancestors, and celebrate the traditions that have been handed down through time. In this way, music and dance serve as a bridge between past and present, linking generations together in a shared appreciation for the cultural richness of the Dolomite region.

Moreover, traditional Dolomite music and dance play a key role in local festivals and celebrations that take place throughout the year. From harvest festivals to religious processions, these events provide opportunities for communities to come together, express their creativity, and showcase their cultural heritage through music and dance. Whether it's a lively street parade or a solemn church ceremony, music and dance are integral components of these festive occasions, adding color, energy, and emotion to the proceedings.

In recent years, efforts have been made to preserve and promote traditional Dolomite music and dance through cultural initiatives, educational programs, and performance opportunities. Local schools, community centers, and cultural organizations offer classes in traditional music and dance to children and adults alike, ensuring that these art forms continue to thrive and evolve in the modern world. Additionally, professional musicians and dancers perform at concerts, festivals, and cultural events both within the region and beyond, sharing the beauty and vitality of Dolomite music and dance with audiences around the world.

Traditional Dolomite music and dance are cherished expressions of culture, history, and community in this picturesque region of northeastern Italy. Through lively tunes, spirited dances, and heartfelt lyrics, the people of the Dolomites celebrate their heritage, connect with one another, and express their unique identity through music and movement. As these traditions continue to be passed down from generation to generation, they will remain an enduring symbol of the enduring spirit and resilience of the Dolomite people.

CHAPTER 9

HEALTH AND SAFETY IN THE DOLOMITES

Emergency Contacts

Emergency contacts are a crucial aspect of personal safety and well-being, providing a lifeline in times of crisis or distress. Whether it's a medical emergency, a natural disaster, or a personal crisis, having reliable emergency contacts can make all the difference in getting the help and support you need when you need it most. In this article, we will explore the importance of emergency contacts, how to choose them wisely, and how to ensure they are readily accessible in case of an emergency.

First and foremost, having designated emergency contacts is essential for ensuring that help can be quickly and efficiently summoned in times of need. These individuals are typically trusted family members, friends, or neighbors who can be relied upon to act swiftly and responsibly in an emergency situation. By designating specific individuals as emergency contacts, you can streamline the process of contacting help and ensure that important information is communicated effectively to the appropriate authorities.

When choosing emergency contacts, it is important to consider several factors to ensure that they are well-suited for the role. Ideally, emergency contacts should be individuals who are familiar with your medical history, allergies, medications, and any other pertinent information that may be relevant in an emergency situation. They should also be easily reachable by phone or email, and willing and able to assist you in times of need.

In addition to family members and friends, it may also be beneficial to include healthcare providers, neighbors, or colleagues as emergency contacts, depending on your individual circumstances. For example, if you have a chronic medical condition or allergy that requires immediate attention, it may be wise to include your primary care physician or specialist as an emergency contact. Similarly, if you live alone or have limited social support, having a trusted neighbor or coworker as an emergency contact can provide an added layer of security and peace of mind.

Once you have identified your emergency contacts, it is important to ensure that they are readily accessible in case of an emergency. This can be accomplished by storing their contact information in multiple locations, such as your phone, wallet, and home address book. Additionally, it may be helpful to provide your emergency contacts with a copy of your medical information, including any relevant health conditions, medications, and allergies, so that they can relay this information to first responders or healthcare providers if necessary.

In today's digital age, there are also a number of smartphone apps and services that allow you to store and access emergency contact information quickly and easily. These apps typically allow you to input multiple emergency contacts, along with important medical information and other relevant details, so that they can be accessed with a few taps on your phone in the event of an emergency. Some apps even offer features such as GPS tracking, which can help emergency responders locate you more quickly in case of an emergency.

In addition to selecting and storing emergency contact information, it is also important to periodically review and update your list of emergency contacts as needed. Life circumstances change, people move, and relationships evolve over time, so it is essential to ensure that your emergency contacts are current and up-to-date. This may involve reaching out to your designated contacts periodically to confirm their willingness to serve in this role and update any changes to their contact information.

Emergency contacts are a vital component of personal safety and preparedness, providing a lifeline in times of crisis and ensuring that help can be quickly summoned when needed. By carefully selecting and storing emergency contact information, you can enhance your ability to respond effectively to emergencies and receive the support and assistance you need in challenging situations. Remember: when it comes to emergencies, having reliable emergency contacts can make all the difference between a positive outcome and a potential disaster.

Healthcare Facilities

Healthcare facilities play a crucial role in providing medical care, treatment, and support to individuals in need of healthcare services. From hospitals and clinics to nursing homes and rehabilitation centers, healthcare facilities encompass a wide range of settings where healthcare professionals work tirelessly to promote health, prevent illness, and treat medical conditions. In this article, we will explore the importance of healthcare facilities, the different types of facilities available, and the key factors that contribute to their effectiveness in delivering quality care to patients.

Healthcare facilities are essential components of the healthcare system, serving as the primary points of access for individuals seeking medical care and treatment. These facilities provide a wide range of services, including primary care, specialty care, diagnostic testing, surgery, rehabilitation, and long-term care, among others. They are staffed by a diverse team of healthcare professionals, including physicians, nurses, therapists, technicians, and support staff, who work together to deliver comprehensive and coordinated care to patients.

One of the key functions of healthcare facilities is to diagnose and treat medical conditions, ranging from common illnesses and injuries to complex and chronic diseases. Hospitals, for example, are equipped with advanced medical technology and specialized medical staff to provide acute care services to patients with serious or life-threatening conditions. Clinics, on the other hand, offer primary care services, such as preventive care, routine check-ups, and management of chronic conditions, to patients in the community.

In addition to diagnosing and treating medical conditions, healthcare facilities also play a critical role in promoting health and wellness through preventive care and health education. Many facilities offer preventive services such as vaccinations, screenings, counseling, and health promotion programs to help individuals maintain good health and prevent the onset of diseases. By emphasizing preventive care and early intervention, healthcare facilities can reduce the burden of disease, improve health outcomes, and lower healthcare costs in the long run.

Healthcare facilities come in various forms and sizes, each catering to specific patient populations and healthcare needs.

Hospitals are the most comprehensive healthcare facilities, offering a wide range of services and specialties to patients with diverse medical needs. They are typically equipped with emergency departments, intensive care units, surgical suites, diagnostic imaging facilities, and inpatient wards to provide round-the-clock care to patients with acute or complex medical conditions.

Clinics are another common type of healthcare facility that provides outpatient care to patients with less severe or chronic medical conditions. These facilities may be operated by individual physicians or group practices and offer services such as primary care, specialty care, diagnostic testing, and minor procedures on an outpatient basis. Clinics are often more accessible and convenient for patients seeking routine or non-emergency medical care.

Other types of healthcare facilities include long-term care facilities, such as nursing homes and assisted living facilities, which provide residential care and support to elderly or disabled individuals who require assistance with activities of daily living. Rehabilitation centers offer specialized services for patients recovering from injuries, surgeries, or illnesses, such as physical therapy, occupational therapy, and speech therapy to help restore function and improve quality of life.

The effectiveness of healthcare facilities in delivering quality care to patients depends on several key factors, including access to care, quality of care, patient safety, coordination of care, and patient satisfaction. Access to care is a critical factor that influences patient outcomes and health disparities, as individuals who face barriers to accessing healthcare services may delay seeking care or receive inadequate treatment. Healthcare facilities must strive to ensure that all patients have timely access to appropriate care that meets their needs.

Quality of care is another essential factor that drives the effectiveness of healthcare facilities in delivering safe and effective treatment to patients. Quality measures such as evidence-based practices, clinical guidelines, patient safety protocols, and performance metrics help healthcare facilities monitor and improve the quality of care they provide. By adhering to best practices and standards of care, healthcare facilities can enhance patient outcomes, reduce medical errors, and improve overall patient satisfaction.

Patient safety is a paramount concern for healthcare facilities, as medical errors and adverse events can have serious consequences for patients' health and well-being. Healthcare facilities must implement robust safety protocols, infection control measures, medication management systems, and risk mitigation strategies to minimize the risk of harm to patients. By prioritizing patient safety and implementing best practices in patient care, healthcare facilities can create a culture of safety that protects patients from preventable harm.

Coordination of care is another critical factor that contributes to the effectiveness of healthcare facilities in providing seamless and integrated care to patients across different settings and specialties. Effective communication among healthcare providers, timely sharing of information, care coordination protocols, and multidisciplinary team-based care models help ensure that patients receive comprehensive and coordinated care that addresses their individual needs. By fostering collaboration among healthcare providers and promoting continuity of care, healthcare facilities can improve patient outcomes and enhance the patient experience.

Patient satisfaction is an important measure of the quality of care provided by healthcare facilities, as it reflects patients' perceptions of their experiences with the healthcare system. Patient satisfaction surveys, feedback mechanisms, and patient engagement initiatives help healthcare facilities gather valuable insights into patients' preferences, concerns, and expectations regarding their care. By listening to patient feedback and incorporating patient-centered approaches into their practice, healthcare facilities can enhance patient satisfaction, build trust with patients, and improve overall quality of care.

Healthcare facilities are essential components of the healthcare system that play a vital role in providing medical care, treatment, and support to individuals in need. By offering a wide range of services, promoting health and wellness through preventive care, and emphasizing quality of care, patient safety, coordination of care, and patient satisfaction, healthcare facilities contribute to improved health outcomes, enhanced patient experiences, and better overall health for communities. As the cornerstone of the healthcare system, healthcare facilities continue to evolve and adapt to meet the changing needs of patients and deliver high-quality care that makes a positive impact on people's lives.

Safety Tips for Travelers

Traveling is an exciting and enriching experience that allows individuals to explore new destinations, cultures, and landscapes. Whether you are embarking on a leisurely vacation, a business trip, or an adventure-filled journey, it is important to prioritize safety and security while traveling to ensure a smooth and enjoyable trip. In this article, we will discuss essential safety tips for travelers to help you stay safe and secure during your travels.

1. Research Your Destination: Before you embark on your trip, take the time to research your destination thoroughly. Learn about the local customs, culture, laws, and potential safety risks in the area. Understand the political climate, health concerns, and any travel advisories issued by your government. By being informed about your destination, you can make informed decisions and avoid potential hazards.

2. Pack Wisely: When packing for your trip, pack light and only bring essential items to avoid attracting unwanted attention and minimize the risk of theft. Keep valuable items such as passports, money, credit cards, and electronic devices in a secure location, such as a money belt or a hidden pocket.

Consider photocopying important documents and keeping digital copies in case of loss or theft.

3. Stay Connected: Make sure to stay connected with family members, friends, or colleagues during your trip. Share your itinerary, contact information, and emergency contacts with someone you trust. Keep your phone charged and carry a portable charger or power bank to ensure you can communicate in case of an emergency.

4. Be Aware of Your Surroundings: When exploring unfamiliar places, be vigilant and aware of your surroundings at all times. Avoid displaying expensive items or flashy jewelry that may attract thieves. Stay alert in crowded areas, public transportation, and tourist attractions where pickpockets may operate. Trust your instincts and avoid risky situations or unsafe areas.

5. Use Reliable Transportation: When traveling from one place to another, use reputable transportation services such as licensed taxis, ride-sharing apps, or public transportation. Avoid accepting rides from strangers or unmarked vehicles to reduce the risk of scams or unsafe situations. Research

transportation options in advance and choose reliable providers with good reviews.

6. Secure Your Accommodations: When booking accommodations, choose reputable hotels, hostels, or vacation rentals with good security measures in place. Lock your doors and windows when inside your room and use the hotel safe to store valuables. Avoid sharing personal information with strangers or leaving your room key unattended.

7. Stay Healthy: Prioritize your health and well-being while traveling by staying hydrated, eating nutritious meals, and getting enough rest. Carry a small first aid kit with essential medications, bandages, and other medical supplies in case of minor injuries or illnesses. Follow food and water safety guidelines to prevent food poisoning or gastrointestinal issues.

8. Protect Your Identity: Safeguard your personal information and identity while traveling by using secure Wi-Fi networks, avoiding public computers for sensitive tasks, and being cautious when sharing personal details online. Use strong passwords for your devices and accounts and consider using a

virtual private network (VPN) for added security when accessing the internet.

9. Respect Local Laws and Customs: Show respect for the local culture, traditions, and laws of the country you are visiting. Familiarize yourself with local customs, dress codes, and etiquette to avoid offending locals or getting into legal trouble. Follow local regulations regarding photography, alcohol consumption, and other activities to stay out of trouble.

10. Stay Informed: Stay informed about current events, weather conditions, natural disasters, and other potential risks that may affect your travel plans. Monitor local news sources, weather updates, and travel advisories issued by authorities to stay informed about any emergencies or disruptions that

Safety should be a top priority for travelers to ensure a smooth and enjoyable travel experience. By following these essential safety tips, you can minimize risks, protect yourself from potential dangers, and stay safe and secure during your travels.

Recommended Apps and Websites for Traveling in the Dolomites

The Dolomites offer a unique and unforgettable travel experience. Whether you are planning a hiking adventure, a ski trip, or a leisurely exploration of the region, having access to the right apps and websites can enhance your travel experience and help you make the most of your time in the Dolomites. In this article, we will discuss some recommended apps and websites for traveling in the Dolomites to help you plan and navigate your trip effectively.

1. Dolomiti Superski App: If you are visiting the Dolomites during the winter season for skiing or snowboarding, the Dolomiti Superski app is a must-have. This app provides real-time information on ski slopes, lift status, weather conditions, and snow reports for over 1,200 kilometers of interconnected ski slopes in the Dolomiti Superski area. You can also use the app to track your ski runs, find restaurants and mountain huts on the slopes, and access interactive trail maps to plan your skiing adventures.

2. Outdooractive App: For hikers, mountain bikers, and outdoor enthusiasts visiting the Dolomites, the Outdooractive

app is an essential tool for planning and navigating outdoor activities. This app offers detailed trail maps, GPS navigation, route suggestions, elevation profiles, and points of interest for hiking, biking, climbing, and other outdoor adventures in the Dolomites. You can use the app to discover new trails, create custom routes, track your activities, and share your outdoor experiences with fellow travelers.

3. Visit Dolomites Website: The Visit Dolomites website is a comprehensive online resource for travelers planning a trip to the Dolomites. This official tourism website provides information on accommodations, activities, events, attractions, transportation options, and travel tips for exploring the Dolomites region. You can use the website to find hotel recommendations, book guided tours, learn about local festivals and cultural events, and access practical information for your trip.

4. Dolomiti.org Website: The Dolomiti.org website is another valuable online resource for travelers seeking information about the Dolomites region. This website offers detailed guides, articles, maps, and travel tips for exploring the natural beauty and cultural heritage of the Dolomites. You can use the

website to learn about hiking trails, mountain refuges, historical sites, scenic drives, and other points of interest in the area.

5. Dolomite Mountains Website: For travelers interested in guided tours, adventure activities, and customized experiences in the Dolomites, the Dolomite Mountains website is a great resource. This specialized tour operator offers a wide range of outdoor adventures, including hiking tours, climbing expeditions, via ferrata excursions, ski trips, and cultural experiences in the Dolomites. You can browse their tour offerings, read about their expert guides, and book tailored experiences to make the most of your time in the region.

6. Dolomiti.org Weather Forecast: Before embarking on outdoor activities in the Dolomites, it is essential to check the weather forecast to ensure a safe and enjoyable experience. The Dolomiti.org website provides up-to-date weather information, including temperature forecasts, precipitation levels, wind speeds, and avalanche risk assessments for different areas in the Dolomites. By staying informed about weather conditions, you can plan your outdoor adventures accordingly and prepare for changing weather patterns.

7. Dolomite Villages App: If you are looking to explore the charming villages and towns scattered throughout the Dolomites region, the Dolomite Villages app can help you discover hidden gems, local attractions, restaurants, shops, and cultural sites in each village. This app provides detailed information on village his

ChatGPT & Midjourney | AI bot, [3/6/24, 10:45 PM]
tory, architecture, traditions, and events to help you immerse yourself in the local culture and experience authentic Dolomite hospitality.

8. Alta Badia App: For visitors exploring the Alta Badia region in the Dolomites, the Alta Badia app is a useful tool for accessing information on ski slopes, hiking trails, mountain huts, restaurants, events, and services in the area. This app offers interactive maps, live webcams, weather updates, event calendars, and special offers for travelers staying in Alta Badia. You can use the app to plan your activities, find dining options, and stay connected with local services during your visit.

Having access to recommended apps and websites can enhance your travel experience in the Dolomites by providing valuable information, navigation tools, activity suggestions, weather updates, and local insights. Whether you are planning a winter ski trip or a summer hiking adventure in this spectacular mountain region, these apps and websites can help you plan your trip effectively, stay informed about local conditions, and make the most of your time exploring the natural beauty and cultural heritage of the Dolomites. With these resources at your fingertips, you can navigate the mountains with confidence and create unforgettable memories during your travels in this enchanting destination.

CONCLUSION

Thank you for choosing to embark on a journey through the breathtaking Dolomites with me as your guide. Your decision to explore this stunning region is one that will surely be filled with unforgettable experiences and awe-inspiring moments. The Dolomites truly are a place like no other, where nature's beauty knows no bounds and where adventure awaits around every corner.

As you flip through the pages of this guidebook, I hope you have found all the information you need to make the most of your time in the Dolomites. From the best hiking trails to the most charming mountain villages, I have strived to provide you with a comprehensive overview of this enchanting destination. But remember, the Dolomites are not just about ticking off sights from a list – they are about immersing yourself in nature, connecting with the local culture, and creating memories that will last a lifetime.

To truly make the most of your time in the Dolomites, I encourage you to embrace the spirit of adventure and exploration. Take the time to wander off the beaten path, to discover hidden gems that are not mentioned in any guidebook. Engage with the locals, learn about their traditions and way of life, and savor the delicious cuisine that is unique to this region. Whether you are an avid hiker, a passionate photographer, or simply someone who appreciates the beauty of nature, there is something in the Dolomites for everyone.

As you set out to explore the Dolomites, remember to always respect the environment and leave no trace behind. The mountains are fragile ecosystems that need to be protected for future generations to enjoy. Take only photographs, leave only footprints, and tread lightly on this precious land.

I wish you safe travels and many unforgettable moments in the Dolomites. May your journey be filled with wonder and joy, and may you return home with a heart full of memories that will last a lifetime. Thank you once again for choosing this guidebook as your companion on this incredible adventure.

Happy exploring, and may the beauty of the Dolomites inspire you in ways you never thought possible. Buon viaggio!

Made in the USA
Middletown, DE
20 May 2024